英美文学经典作品
赏析与导读

美国篇

郑野　李雯　主编

中国出版集团
世界图书出版公司

图书在版编目（CIP）数据

英美文学经典作品赏析与导读. 美国篇/郑野，李雯主编. —广州：世界图书出版广东有限公司，2015. 6
ISBN 978-7-5100-9695-2

Ⅰ. ①英…　Ⅱ. ①郑…　②李…　Ⅲ. ①英语—阅读教学—高等学校—教材　②文学欣赏—美国　Ⅳ. ①H319.4：I

中国版本图书馆CIP数据核字（2015）第110964号

英美文学经典作品赏析与导读（美国篇）

项目策划：刘正武
责任编辑：张　华
出版发行：世界图书出版广东有限公司
（广州市新港西路大江冲25号　邮编：510300）
电　　话：（020）84451969　84453623　84184026　84459579
http：//www.gdst.com.cn　E-mail：pub@gdst.com.cn
经　　销：各地新华书店
印　　刷：虎彩印艺股份有限公司
版　　次：2015年8月第1版
印　　次：2016年3月第2次印刷
开　　本：787mm × 1092mm　1/16
印　　张：10.75
字　　数：167千
ISBN 978-7-5100-9695-2/I·0350
定　　价：30.00元

咨询、投稿：020-84460251　gzlzw@126.com

前　言

严格地说，美国文学的形成应从美国立国开始。但实际上，在此以前一二百年的殖民时期的文学虽然并不发达，主要以模仿为主，没有自己鲜明的特色，但那时的政治、经济和社会的发展对美国文学的形成还是有很大的影响的。例如，由于殖民者大量屠杀原来居住在北美大陆的印第安人，使他们的文化和民间口头文学的传统受到致命的摧残，因此美国文学没有英国《贝奥武甫》那样的口头文学遗产。另一方面，当年来美洲大陆移民的人基本上属于两种人，一类是为了逃避国内政治迫害、追求宗教自由的英国清教徒，他们来到新英格兰地区扎根发展，另一类是谋求发财致富的欧洲老百姓，包括野心勃勃的冒险家。不论哪一种人都相信在新大陆都可以得到自由平等，都有机会实现自己的理想。这种观点使“美国梦”成为日后美国文学的一个永恒的主题。清教主义有关人生来有罪及上帝主宰一切等思想也影响着美国作家不断地思考人性与原罪、人与上帝的关系。作为一个由移民组成的国家，美国受各种文化的影响。这又决定了美国文学要比其他西方文学更具有多样性。

美国文学的历史不长，但发展较快，20世纪以来，在世界上的影响越来越大。我国早在19世纪70年代就翻译了朗费罗的《人生颂》(*A Psalm of Life*)。1901年，林抒翻译出版了第一部美国小说——斯托人的《黑奴吁录》(*Uncle Tom's Cabin*，今译《汤姆叔叔的小屋》)，在读者中引起极大的震动，使他们从黑奴身上看到自己亡国灭种的危险。根据小说改编的话剧对我们话剧运动的发展也起到了很大的作用。五四运动前后，惠特曼对郭沫若等诗人、奥尼尔对曹禺、洪深等戏剧家都产生过影响。马克·吐温、辛克莱、德莱塞等人都曾受到鲁迅等左翼作家的好评。改革开放以来，美国文学对我国新时期的作家们有着巨大的吸引力。盛行一时的朦胧诗恐怕就是在美国及西方现代派诗歌的影响下产生的。海明威、福克纳及塞林格等人几乎成为我们年轻一代作家文学创作的楷模。至于在世界上，埃德加·爱伦·坡曾被法国象征派诗人称为他们的诗歌之父，福克纳对法国的萨特和加缪以及拉丁美洲的加西亚·马尔克斯的影响也是有目共睹的事实。美国作家喜爱描述初涉人世、寻求生活道路和人生真谛的“成长小说”，此类文体形式受到加拿大女作家的欣赏，也正在被我国的儿童文学作家所采用。美国作家的探索、试验、创新的精神也激励着世界各国的作家不断革新，超越前人。今天，在改革开放的时代，在我们加强跟美国交往的时候，我们有必要学一点美国文学，了解他们的文化以促进与美国人民的交流、沟通和理解，同时也借以丰富我们的知识，充实我们的文化修养，提高我们的精神素质。

本套丛书为读者奉上原汁原味的人文阅读精华，其或选自原典正文、专业教材，或选自网络热点、文学史纲目，由精研此业者掇菁撷华、辑录成册，希望能帮助读者在学习英语的同时助其领略西方人文经典的独特魅力。书稿中的学术见解和经典名句均转引自陶洁教授主编的《美国文学选读》(高等教育出版社，2001年版)，特此说明。

文学共语言同飞，阅读与思想共舞。让我们在书页和文字之间体味大千世界的真谛，在原汁原味的英语经典阅读中品文化、学英语、长知识，并在分享人类文明的过程中成就自己的文化修养、人文理念及完美人生。

郑野　李雯

2015年3月于郑州龙子湖畔

目 录

第一章
本杰明·富兰克林Benjamin Franklin

作者简介

本杰明·富兰克林(Benjamin Franklin, 1706—1790)，作家、科学家、政治家、发明家。出身低微，10岁起受过两年的小学教育，12岁开始在印刷厂当学徒，但利用业余时间刻苦自学，除母语之外，还能够熟练地阅读法语、西班牙语、意大利语和拉丁语著作。16岁开始在《新英格兰周报》发表小品文，评论时务。24岁成为印刷厂的业主后，致力于社会公共事业，先后创建费城公共图书馆，主编《宾夕法尼亚报》，还于1751年协助创办了宾夕法尼亚大学。中年之后，他发奋研究物理、化学、数学、天文学等自然科学，取得了重要成就。后成为美国革命中的核心人物之一，参与起草《独立宣言》。1776年至1785年，他作为美国的全权代表出使法国，寻求欧洲盟友在政治、经济、军事等方面的支持和援助，出色地完成了使命。富兰克林一生著述丰富，内容涉及时政、科学、经济、教育、个人生活阅历等诸多方面。1732年，他用笔名发表了《格言历书》(*Poor Richard's Almanac*)，内容除历书之外还附有谚语、格言、警句，非常畅销，后作为系列出版物发行25年。他的《自传》(*The Autobiography*)著于1771年至1790年，生动而深刻地记载了他个人的生活经历，历来被公认为美国文学的经典之作。

内容提要

选篇出自《自传》第一章。1771年，时年65岁的富兰克林在英国回忆自己前半生的生活经历，并以“自传”的形式记载下来，以传后人。《自传》的写作前后历时近20年。该书共由四个部分组成，第一部分主要讲述了他一生前25年的生活经历，包括短暂的学校读书生活、在印刷厂的学徒经历、如何在艰苦的环境中勤奋自学、匿名为报纸撰稿，以及开始在印刷业获得成功并结婚成家。1784年，第二部分成文于巴黎，侧重描写作者在科学研究方面的兴趣和成就，还涉及到他所从事的社会公共事业。第三、四两个部分分别在1788 年、1789年至1790年写于富兰克林的家乡费城，先后记叙了他从25岁至51岁的生活。至于作者后半生33 年的生活，尤其是在欧洲和本国政界、外交界的经历和成就，作者只是在最后两个部分略有提及。换言之，《自传》并非作者一生完整的传记。富兰克林去世后，该书的部分章节未经授权曾在法国和英国出版，文字及内容均有失实之处，全部手稿直至1868年在巴黎发现后，才在当年出版了该书最为完整的版本。

赏 析

《自传》不仅是美国第一部成功的传记体作品，而且也是美国民族文学的早期代表作。自1868年全书问世之后，其价值和影响经久不衰。对于这部在美国文学史上占有重要地位的作品，可以从若干不同的视角解读和赏析。从传记文学的角度来说,《自传》的作者是一位土生土长的美国人，出身寒微，没有受过良好的正规教育，没有浪漫的爱情，没有权贵的提携，完全借助于自己不懈的努力而获得了成功。这有别于欧洲文学中传统的传记作品，不像它们以君王、重臣或者英雄为主人公，描写远离普通人见识的经历，字里行间充满了宫廷争斗、颠覆夺权、战争杀戮、神秘莫测的命运以及政治化事件。在富兰克林的笔下，一个原本普通的美国平民逐步从幼年走向青年和成年，从幼稚变得成熟，从致力于工业过渡到投身科学研究，从个人奋斗转而为国家的独立发挥重要作用，而他所经历的所有一切，都是平凡而简单的生活故事。他之所以成功，一方面依靠自身的勤奋和信念的力量，另一方面还在于时代的造就。但是对于18世纪前半叶美国相对自由、宽松的社会环境，富兰克林并没有着力渲染，而是将其作为一种背景衬托他个人的成长历程。

《自传》不仅描写了一个成功者在美国建国前期取得的成就，其价值和意义还在于揭示这一人物内在道德品性的塑造过程。清教主义中勤奋、务实、上进的精神，以及启蒙时期美国人民对于自己民族未来发展的想象与信心，都凝聚于他的个性之中，从而表现为一种强大的生命活力。富兰克林以此为自豪，而且自觉地设法将其道德伦理信念传达给读者。这一点明显见于书中的第二、三、四部分。作为一个典型的美国人的写照，《自传》展示了18世纪美国的社会图景以及启蒙时代的精神风貌，塑造了一个全新的美国人的形象，并以个人的发展和成就再现了社会孕育的活力。对于美国民族个性的形成，这一人物形象起到了重要而长久的影响，同时也在一定程度上开始扭转欧洲人对美国人的蔑视与偏见。

从叙事语言来看，《自传》真实感人，个性化的文笔洗练清新，风格纯朴，少有18世纪英国乃至整个欧洲文坛所崇尚的雕琢的文风。但在该书的四个部分中，显然富兰克林心目中拥有不同的读者，因此各个部分的叙事风格也有所差异。在第一部分，富兰克林以“亲爱的儿子”开篇，读者为他的后嗣，纯朴亲切的字句可以使人领略到父子深情。从第二部分开始，读者以社会人众为对象，作者与读者之间的对话开始保持一定的距离，说教的意味也溢于字面。此外，由于《自传》写作的时间漫长，各个部分只是按照时间顺序衔接，在叙事结构上略显松散。

The Autobiography[1]

(Excerpt)

TO HIS SON

Twyford[2], at the Bishop of St. Asaph's, 1771

Dear Son[3],

I have ever had a pleasure in obtaining any little anecdotes of my ancestors. You may remember the enquiries I made among the remains of my relations[4] when you were with me in England and the journey I undertook for that purpose.

Imagining it may be equally agreeable to you to know the circumstances of my Life—many of which you are yet unacquainted with—and expecting a week's uninterrupted Leisure in my present country retirement, I sit down to write them for you. Besides, there are some other inducements that excite me to this undertaking. From the poverty and obscurity in which I was born and in which I passed my earliest years, I have raised myself to a state of affluence[5] and some degree of celebrity in the world. As constant good fortune has accompanied me even to an advanced period of life, my posterity will perhaps be desirous of learning the means, which I employed, and which, thanks to Providence[6], so well succeeded with me. They may also deem them fit to be Imitated, should any of them find themselves in similar circumstances. That good fortune, when I reflected on it, which is frequently the case, has induced me sometimes to say that were it left to my choice, I should have no objection to go over the same life from its beginning to the end, only asking the advantage authors have of correcting in a second edition some faults of the first. So would I also wish to change some incidents of it for others more favourable. Notwithstanding, if this condition were denied, I should still accept the offer. But as this repetition is not to be expected, that which resembles most living one's life over again, seems to be to recall all the circumstances of it; and, to render this remembrance more durable, to record them in writing, in thus employing myself I shall yield to the inclination so natural to old men of talking of themselves and their own actions, and I shall indulge it, without being tiresome to those who, from respect to my age, might conceive themselves obliged to listen to me, since they will be always free to read me or not. And lastly (I may as well confess it, as the denial of it would be believed by nobody) I shall perhaps not a little gratify my own vanity. Indeed, I never heard or saw the introductory words, "Without Vanity I may say," etc., but some vain thing immediately followed. Most people dislike vanity in others whatever share they have of it themselves, but I give it fair quarter[7] wherever I meet with it, being persuaded that it is often productive of good to the possessor and to others who are within his sphere of action. And therefore, in many cases it would not be altogether absurd if a man were to thank God for his vanity among the other comforts of life. And now I speak of thanking God, I desire with all humility to acknowledge that I owe the mentioned happiness of my past life to his divine providence, which led me to the means I used and gave them success. My belief of this induces me to hope, though I must not presume, that the same goodness will still be exercised towards me in continuing that happiness or in enabling me to bear a fatal reverse, which I may experience as others have done—the complexion of my future fortune being known to him only, and in whose power it is to bless to us even our afflictions.

THE ARRIVAL IN PHILADELPHIA

[Following the altercation with his older brother to whom Franklin had been apprenticed (and whose oppressive treatment of Franklin, the latter says, gave him "that aversion to arbitrary power that has stuck to me through my whole life"), and after a brush with the law, the seventeen-year-old lad leaves Boston and comes to Philadelphia, the city whose first citizen he would eventually become.]

This might be one occasion of the differences we[8] began to have about this time. Though a brother, he considered himself as my master and me as his apprentice, and accordingly expected the same services from me as he would from another; while I thought he degraded me too much in some he required of me, who from a brother expected more indulgence. Our disputes were often brought before our father, and I fancy I was either generally in the right or else a better pleader, because the judgment was generally in my favour. But my brother was passionate and had often beaten me, which I took extremely amiss. I fancy his harsh and tyrannical treatment of me might be a means of impressing me with that aversion to arbitrary power that has stuck to me through my whole life. Thinking my apprenticeship very tedious, I was continually wishing for some opportunity of shortening it, which at length offered in a manner unexpected.

One of the pieces in our newspaper on some political point which I have now forgotten, gave offence to the Assembly[9]. He was taken up, censured, and imprisoned for a month by the Speaker's warrant, I suppose because he would not discover the author. I, too, was taken up and examined before the Council; but though I did not give them any satisfaction, they contented themselves with admonishing me and dismissed me, considering me, perhaps, as an apprentice who was bound to keep his master's secrets. During my brother's confinement, which I resented a good deal notwithstanding our private differences, I had the management of the paper, and I made bold to give our rulers some rubs in it, which my brother took very kindly, while others began to consider me in an unfavourable light as a young genius that had a turn for libelling and satire. My brother's discharge was accompanied with an order from the House (a very odd one) that "James Franklin should no longer print the paper called the New England Courant." There was a consultation held in our printing house amongst his friends in this conjuncture. Some proposed to elude the order by changing the name of the paper; but my brother seeing inconveniences in that, it was finally concluded on as a better way to let it be printed for the future under the name of "Benjamin Franklin" ; and to avoid the censure of the Assembly that might fall on him as still printing it by his apprentice, the contrivance was that my old indenture[10] should be returned to me with a full discharge on the back of it, to show in case of necessity; but to secure to him the benefit of my service, I should sign new indentures for the remainder of the term, which were to be kept private. A very flimsy[11] scheme it was, but, however, it was immediately executed, and the paper went on accordingly under my name for several months. At length a fresh difference arising between my brother and me, I took upon me to assert my freedom, presuming that he would not venture to produce the new indentures. It was not fair in me to take this advantage, and this I therefore reckon one of the first errata[12] of my life. But the unfairness of it weighed little with me, when under the impressions of resentment for the blows his passion too often urged him to bestow upon me, though he was otherwise not an ill-natured man. Perhaps I was too saucy and provoking.

When he found I would leave him, he took care to prevent my getting employment in any other printing house of the town by going round and speaking to every master, who accordingly refused to give me work. I then thought of going to New York as the nearest place where there was a printer; and I was the rather inclined to leave Boston when I reflected that I had already made myself a little obnoxious[13] to the governing party; and from the arbitrary proceedings of the Assembly in my brother's case, it was likely I might if I stayed soon bring myself into scrapes, and further that my indiscreet disputations about religion began to make me pointed at with horror by good people as an infidel or atheist. I determined on the point, but my father now siding with my brother, I was sensible that if I attempted to go openly, means would be used to prevent me. My friend Collins therefore undertook to manage my flight. He agreed with the captain of a New York sloop for my passage, under pretence of my being a young man of his acquaintance that had had an intrigue with a girl of bad character, whose parents would compel me to marry her and therefore I could not appear or come away publicly. I sold some of my books to raise a little money, was taken on board the sloop privately, had a fair wind, and in three days found myself at New York, near three hundred miles from my home, at the age of seventeen, without the least recommendation to or knowledge of any person in the place, and with very little money in my pocket.

The inclination I had had for the sea was by this time done away, or I might now have gratified it. But having another profession and conceiving myself a pretty good workman, I offered my services to the printer of the place, old Mr. Wm. Bradford (who had been the first printer in Pennsylvania, but had removed thence in consequence of a quarrel with the Governor, Geo. Keith). He could give me no employment, having little to do and hands enough already. "But," says he, "my son at Philadelphia has lately lost his principal hand, Aquila Rose, by death. If you go thither I believe he may employ you."

Philadelphia was a hundred miles farther. I set out, however, in a boat for Amboy[14], leaving my chest and things to follow me round by sea. In crossing the bay we met with a squall that tore our rotten sails to pieces, prevented our getting into the kill, and drove us upon Long Island. In our way a drunken Dutchman, who was a passenger, too, fell overboard; when he was sinking, reached through the water to his shock pate and drew him up so that we got him in again. His ducking sobered him a little, and he went to sleep, taking first out of his pocket a book which he desired I would dry for him. It proved to be my old favourite author Bunyan's Pilgrim's Progress[15] in Dutch, finely printed on good paper with copper cuts, a dress better than I had ever seen it wear in its own language. I have since found that it has been translated into most of the languages of Europe, and suppose it has been more generally read than any other book except, perhaps, the Bible. Honest John[16] was the first that I know of who mixes narration and dialogue, a method of writing very engaging to the reader, who in the most interesting parts finds himself, as it were, admitted into the company and present at the conversation. Defoe[17] has imitated him successfully in his Robinson Crusoe[18], in his Moll Flanders[19], and other pieces; and Richardson has done the same in his Pamela[20], etc.

On approaching the island, we found it was in a place where there could be no landing, there being a great surf on the stony beach. So we dropped anchor and swung out our cable towards the shore. Some people came down to the water edge and hallooed to us, as we did to them, but the wind was so high and the surf so loud that we could not understand each other. There were some canoes on the shore, and we made signs and called to them to fetch us, but they either did not comprehend us or thought it impracticable so they went off. Night approaching, we had no remedy but to have patience till the wind abated, and in the meantime the boatman and I concluded to sleep if we could, and so we crowded into the scuttle[21] with the Dutchman who was still wet, and the spray breaking over the head of our boat leaked through to us, so that we were soon almost as wet as he. In this manner we lay all night with very little rest; but the wind abating the next day, we made a shift to reach Amboy before night, having been thirty hours on the water without victuals or any drink but a bottle of filthy rum, the water we sailed on being salt.

In the evening I found myself very feverish and went to bed; but having read somewhere that cold water drank plentifully was good for a fever, I followed the prescription, sweat plentifully most of the night, my fever left me, and in the morning crossing the ferry, I proceeded on my journey on foot, having fifty miles to Burlington[22], where I was told I should find boats that would carry me the rest of the way to Philadelphia.

It rained very hard all the day, I was thoroughly soaked and by noon a good deal tired, so I stopped at a poor inn, where I stayed all night, beginning now to wish I had never left home. I made so miserable a figure, too, that I found by the questions asked me I was suspected to be some run-away servant, and in danger of being taken up on that suspicion. However, I proceeded the next day, and got in the evening to an inn within eight or ten miles of Burlington, kept by one Dr. Brown[23].

He entered into conversation with me while I took some refreshment and, finding I had read a little, became very sociable and friendly. Our acquaintance continued all the rest of his life. He had been, I imagine, an itinerant doctor, for there was no town in England or any country in Europe of which he could not give a very particular account. He had some letters and was ingenious, but he was an infidel and wickedly undertook some years after to travesty the Bible in doggerel verse as Cotton had done with Virgil[24]. By this means he set many of the facts in a very ridiculous light and might have done mischief with weak minds if his work had been published, but it never was. At his house I lay that night, and the next morning reached Burlington, but had the mortification to find that the regular boats were gone a little before and no other expected to go before Tuesday, this being Saturday. Wherefore[25], I returned to an old woman in the town of whom I had bought some gingerbread[26] to eat on the water and asked her advice; she invited me to lodge at her house till a passage by water should offer; and being tired with my foot travelling, I accepted the invitation. Understanding I was a printer, she would have had me remain in that town and follow my business, being ignorant of the stock necessary to begin with. She was very hospitable, gave me a dinner of ox cheek with great goodwill, accepting only of a pot of ale in return. And I thought myself fixed till Tuesday should come. However, walking in the evening by the side of the river, a boat came by, which I found was going towards Philadelphia with several people in her. They took me in, and as there was no wind, we rowed all the way; and about midnight, not having yet seen the city, some of the company were confident we must have passed it and would row no farther; the others knew not where we were, so we put towards the shore, got into a creek, landed near an old fence, with the rails of which we made a fire, the night being cold in October, and there we remained till daylight. Then one of the company knew the place to be Cooper's Creek, a little above Philadelphia, which we saw as soon as we got out of the creek, and arrived there about eight or nine o'clock, on the Sunday morning and landed at the Market Street wharf.

I have been the more particular in this description of my journey, and shall be so of my first entry into that city, that you may in your mind compare such unlikely beginnings with the figure I have since made there. I was in my working dress, my best clothes being to come round by sea. I was dirty from my journey; my pockets were stuffed out with shirts and stockings; I knew no soul, nor where to look for lodging. Fatigued with walking, rowing, and want of sleep, I was very hungry, and my whole stock of cash consisted of a Dutch dollar and about a shilling in copper coin, which I gave to the boatmen for my passage. At first they refused it on account of my having rowed, but I insisted on their taking it. A man is sometimes more generous when he has little money than when he has plenty, perhaps through fear of being thought to have but little. I walked towards the top of the street, gazing about till near Market Street, where I met a boy with bread. I have often made a meal of dry bread, and inquiring where he had bought it, I went immediately to the baker's he directed me to. I asked for biscuit, meaning such as we had in Boston, but that sort, it seems, was not made in Philadelphia. I then asked for a threepenny loaf and was told they had none such. Not knowing the different prices nor the names of the different sorts of any bread, I told him to give me three pennyworth of any sort. He gave me accordingly three great puffy rolls. I was surprised at the quantity but took it, and having no room in my pockets, walked off with a roll under each arm and eating the other. Thus I went up Market Street as far as Fourth Street, passing by the door of Mr. Read, my future wife's father, when she, standing at the door, saw me, and thought I made -as I certainly did—a most awkward, ridiculous appearance. Then I turned and went down Chestnut Street and part of Walnut Street, eating my roll all the way, and coming round, found myself again at Market Street wharf near the boat I came in, to which I went for a draught of the river water, and being filled with one of my rolls, gave the other two to a woman and her child that came down the river in the boat with us and were waiting to go farther. Thus refreshed, I walked again up the street, which by this time had many clean dressed people in it who were all walking the same way; I joined them, and thereby was led into the great meetinghouse of the Quakers[27] near the market. I sat down among them, and after looking round awhile and hearing nothing said, being very drowsy through labour and want of rest the preceding night, I fell fast asleep and continued so till the meeting broke up, when someone was kind enough to rouse me. This was therefore the first house I was in or slept in, in Philadelphia.

Questions:

1. Why did Franklin write his Autobiography?
2. What made Franklin decide to leave the brother to whom he had been apprenticed?
3. How did he arrive in Philadelphia?
4. What features do you find in the style of the above selection?

注　释

1. 选篇节自《自传》的第一部分，其一为该书的开场白，其二描述富兰克林离开哥哥初到费城时的情形。1723年，17岁的富兰克林两手空空、独自一人来到费城，这是他逐步走向成功的一个重要转折点。
2. Twyford：伦敦西南约50英里处的一个村落。富兰克林在此写作《自传》的第一部分。
3. Dear Son：指富兰克林的儿子威廉·富兰克林（1731—1813），当时任新泽西州州长。但在独立战争中，威廉·富兰克林是忠于英国的保皇派。
4. the remains of my relations：仍然健在的亲属。1758年，富兰克林曾携子访问祖先在英国的故乡。
5. affluence：富裕；充足。
6. Providence：上帝；神。
7. but I give it fair quarter：但我却公平地对待它。
8. we：指富兰克林和他的哥哥。他当时给哥哥做学徒。
9. the Assembly：马萨诸塞州议会的众议院。
10. indenture：师徒合同；定期服务契约。
11. flimsy：不足以使人有信心的；薄弱的。

12. errata：erratum复数形式，指书写或者印刷中的错误。此处，这一专业术语指人生中出现的失误。
13. obnoxious：讨厌的；令人厌恶的。
14. Amboy：地名，位于新泽西州。
15. Bunyan's Pilgrim's Progress：英国作家约翰·班扬（John Bunyan, 1628—1688）的讽喻小说《天路历程》。
16. Honest John：指英国小说家班扬。
17. Defoe：英国小说家笛福（Daniel Defoe, 约1660—1731）。
18. Robinson Crusoe：笛福的小说《鲁宾逊漂流记》。
19. Moll Flanders：笛福的小说《摩尔·弗兰德斯》。
20. Richardson has done the same in his Pamela, etc.指英国作家理查逊（Samuel Richardson, 1689—1761）以及他的书信体小说《帕美勒》。
21. scuttle：小舱口；舷窗；船底孔洞。
22. Burlington：费城北面约18英里的一个城市，当时为新泽西州的州政府所在地。
23. Dr. Brown：Dr. John Brown（约1667—1737），旅馆的老板，也是当地有名的医生和无神论者。
24. to travesty the Bible in doggerel verse as Cotton had done with Virgil：蹩脚地将《圣经》变为打油诗，就如同科顿拙劣地模仿维吉尔的作品那样。Cotton,即Charles Cotton（1630—1687），英国诗人，曾模仿维吉尔的《埃涅伊德》创作了诗作《斯卡龙尼德》。Virgil：古罗马诗人（公元前70—前19），主要作品为史诗《埃涅伊德》（Aeneid）。
25. wherefore：因此；所以。
26. gingerbread：姜饼；华而不实的东西。
27. the Quakers：（基督教的一个教派）贵格会教徒。该教会由英国人乔治·福克斯（George Fox, 1624—1691）创立，他主张将"内心之光"，即灵感，置于圣经和教条之上，反对繁琐的、程式化的宗教仪式，因此受到宗教当局与政府的双重迫害。

第二章
埃德加·爱伦·坡Edgar Allan Poe

作者简介

埃德加·爱伦·坡（Edgar Allan Poe, 1809-1849），小说家、诗人、批评家。幼年时父母双亡，由商人约翰·爱伦收养为义子。1815年至1820年，他在伦敦读小学，后返回美国在弗吉尼亚大学、西点军校读书。1831年因违反校规被西点军校除名。此后，他一度以出卖文稿谋生，始终为生活的贫困所扰，后曾担任《南方文学使者》等多家刊物的编辑或评论家。1847年妻子病故，他颇为悲伤，不能自已，1849年因酗酒丧生。自青少年开始，他便对文学表现出浓厚的兴趣，阅览了大量的作品，而且很早显露出创作的天分。1827年，他自费出版了第一部诗集《帖木尔》（Tamerlane and Other Poems），随后出版的诗集包括《艾尔·阿拉夫》（Al Araaf, 1829）、《诗集》（Poems, 1831）和《乌鸦及其他诗篇》（The Raven and Other Poems, 1845）。他的诗歌《乌鸦》1845年问世后，受到普遍好评，他的诗才也由此得到了社会的认同。与诗歌相比，他在短篇小说方面的成就更为显著，尤其长于创作哥特式小说和侦探小说，作品主要收入《述异集》（Tales of the Grotesque and Arabesque, 1840）与《故事集》（Tales, 1845）。其中的名篇有《厄舍古厦的倒塌》（"The Fail of the House of Usher"）、《红色死亡假面舞会》（"The Masque of the Red Death"）、《莉盖亚》（"Ligeia"）、《黑猫》（"The Black Cat"）、《阿芒提拉多的酒桶》（"The Cask of Amontinado"）、《莫格街谋杀案》（"Murders in the Rue Morgue"）、《被窃的信件》（"The Purloined Letter"）和《金甲虫》（"The Gold Bug"）。他的侦探小说历来为人称道，一般认为他是西方侦探小说的开山鼻祖。在文学理论方面，他也有不可忽视的建树，鼓吹"纯艺术"的文学价值观，主要理论著作包括《创作哲学》（"The Philosophy of Composition"，1846）和《诗歌原理》（"The Poetic Principle"，1850）。

赏 析

与其同时代的小说家相比，爱伦·坡有许多与众不同之处。其中，最主要的方面之一是他既拥有自己较为系统的创作理论，又能够将其理论付诸于创作实践并取得了非凡的成就。按照他的理论，小说应当着力展示人的内心世界，尤其是人格中以往被忽视的病态或者阴暗的方面，而且叙事要简洁明了，力争使故事以较快的节奏发展到高潮，以便产生某种单一的预期效果。作为其短篇小说佳作之一，《阿芒提拉多的酒桶》体现了他的小说创作艺术的基本特征。

小说的主题是爱伦·坡惯于描写的恐怖和死亡。小说的背景为意大利，以第一人称讲述了主人公蒙特利瑟复仇的故事。小说开篇，蒙特利瑟决计找机会报复弗图纳多。狂欢节期间的一天，弗图纳多畅饮后酩酊大醉，穿戴得像游行队伍中的小丑一样。蒙特利瑟把握住了这个机会，告诉弗图纳多说：他购买了一桶阿芒提拉多酒，但是不能肯定是否真是这一著名品牌的酒。弗图纳多听后，执意要去鉴别酒的真伪。蒙特利瑟佯装推托不过，便带领弗图纳多来到自家的酒窖，引导到最深处的地窖后，旋即将其捆绑在一根事先准备好的铁桩上，接着用石头砌起一道墙，将酒窖的门堵死。弗图纳多终于明白过来，但为时已晚。

事件发生的地点选择在深邃、阴森的酒窖，仅有的两个人物都存在人格上的缺陷。在作者的笔下，弗图纳多的缺陷呈现在明处，而蒙特利瑟的缺陷则是隐匿的。刻画这种区别的意图，在于强化故事结尾的高潮到来时应有的恐怖效果。弗图纳多趾高气扬，目空蒙特利瑟，直到垂死时才霍然醒悟，认识到自己的愚蠢，但只能在绝望和痛苦中等待死亡的到来，歇斯底里的嚎叫改变不了他的命运。蒙特利瑟却自始至终清楚地知道将要发生的一切，他所希望看到的就是弗图纳多的死亡，却以虚伪的谦卑掩盖住了自己的意图。小说还暗示蒙特利瑟在杀人后可以逍遥法外，因为按照他的盘算，无人能知晓他的所作所为。小说的聚焦点正是从蒙特利瑟的老谋深算反衬出来的人格中更深层次的缺陷。他比弗图纳多更邪恶，更可怕，没有节制的复仇欲望完全毁坏了他的灵魂。

小说追求一种篇幅短小而节奏很快的叙事风格，从而使故事迅速到达高潮。为此，作者采取了许多巧妙而有效的方法。首先是削减背景信息，全篇只有开头的一句话交代背景：蒙特利瑟声言弗图纳多曾经多次严重地伤害过他，他出于无奈只能默默地忍受，但是却发誓要寻找机会报复。显而易见，他已经经历了漫长的筹划和等待的过程。至于人物的年龄、身材、容貌、职业、家庭状况等等，只字未提，甚至连故事发生的时间和地点都没有说明，只有“豪华的宫殿（paiazzo）”等几个词的意大利文化背景，提示故事可能发生在意大利。

爱伦·坡主张，在一首诗，或者一篇故事中，每一个字、每一句话、每一个细节都必须有助于实现整个作品的预期效果。可以说，这部小说语言凝练，没有一个字是多余的，没有一句是冗言，没有一个细节是可有可无的。比如，蒙特利瑟脱口而出的拉丁语，虽然只是只言片语，却反映了他接受教育的程度，并且自然而然地使他的文化修养与其残酷的报复形成强烈的对比。此外，作品中象征手法的使用也别具特色，例如，随着蒙特利瑟诱使弗图纳多向酒窖的深处走去，由于缺氧，火把的火光逐渐变小，加之酒桶四周的骷髅似乎也愈来愈多，预示弗图纳多存活的希望愈来愈小。如果将这部小说与《厄舍古厦的倒塌》和《莉盖亚》等同类作品参照阅读，可能会有助于把握上述艺术特色。

The Cask of Amontillado

The thousand injuries of Fortunato I had borne as I best could, but when he ventured upon insult I vowed revenge. You, who so well know the nature of my soul, will not suppose, I however, that I gave utterance to a threat. At length I would be avenged; this was a point definitively settled—but the very definitiveness with which it was resolved precluded the idea of risk. I must not only punish but punish with impunity[1]. A wrong is unredressed when retribution overtakes its redresser. It is equally unredressed when the avenger fails to make himself felt as such to him who has done the wrong. It must be understood that neither by word nor deed had I given Fortunato cause to doubt my good will. I continued, as was my wont, to smile in his face, and he did not perceive that my smile now was at the thought of his immolation.

He had a weak point—this Fortunato—although in other regards he was a man to be respected and even feared. He prided himself upon his connoisseurship in wine. Few Italians have the true virtuoso spirit. For the most part their enthusiasm is adopted to suit the time and opportunity, to practice imposture upon the British and Austrian millionaires. In painting and gemmary, Fortunato, like his countrymen, was a quack[2], but in the matter of old wines he was sincere. In this respect I did not differ from him materially—I was skilful in the Italian vintages myself, and bought largely whenever I could.

It was about dusk, one evening during the supreme madness of the carnival season, that I encountered my friend. He accosted me with excessive warmth, for he had been drinking much. The man wore motley[3]. He had on a tight-fitting parti-striped dress, and his head was surmounted by the conical cap and bells. I was so pleased to see him that I thought I should never have done wringing his hand.

I said to him—"My dear Fortunato, you are luckily met. How remarkably well you are looking today. But I have received a pipe of what passes for Amontillado[4], and I have my doubts." "How?" said he. "Amontillado? A pipe? Impossible! And in the middle of the carnival!"

"I have my doubts," I replied; "and I was silly enough to pay the full Amontillado price without consulting you in the matter. You were not to be found, and I was fearful of losing a bargain." "Amontillado!"

"I have my doubts."

"Amontillado!"

"And I must satisfy them."

"Amontillado!"

"As you are engaged, I am on my way to Luchresi. If any one has a critical turn it is he. He will tell me—"

"Luchresi cannot tell Amontillado from Sherry."

"And yet some fools will have it that his taste is a match for your own."

"Come, let us go."

"Whithe—r?"

"To your vaults."

"My friend, no; I will not impose upon your good nature. I perceive you have an engagement. Luchresi—

"I have no engagement; —come."

"My friend, no. It is not the engagement, but the severe cold with which I perceive you are afflicted. The vaults are insufferably damp. They are encrusted with nitre[5]."

"Let us go, nevertheless. The cold is merely nothing. Amontillado! You have been imposed upon. And as for Luchresi, he cannot distinguish Sherry from Amontillado."

Thus speaking, Fortunato possessed himself of my arm; and putting on a mask of black silk and drawing a roquelaire[6] closely about my person, I suffered him to hurry me to my palazzo[7]. There were no attendants at home; they had absconded to make merry in honour of the time. I had told them that I should not return until the morning, and had given them explicit orders not to stir from the house. These orders were sufficient, I well knew, to insure their immediate disappearance, one and all, as soon as my back was turned.

I took from their sconces two flambeaux, and giving one to Fortunato, bowed him through several suites of rooms to the archway that led into the vaults. I passed down a long and winding staircase, requesting him to be cautious as he followed. We came at length to the foot of the descent, and stood together upon the damp ground of the catacombs of the Montresors. The gait of my friend was unsteady, and the bells upon his cap jingled as he strode.

"The pipe," said he.

"It is farther on," said I; "but observe the white web-work which gleams from these cavern walls."

He turned towards me, and looked into my eyes with two filmy orbs that distilled the rheum of intoxication.

"Nitre?" he asked, at length.

"Nitre," I replied. "How long have you had that cough?"

"Ugh! ugh! ugh!—ugh! ugh! ugh!—ugh! ugh !ugh!—ugh! ugh! ugh!—ugh! ugh! ugh! "

My poor friend found it impossible to reply for many minutes.

"It is nothing," he said, at last.

"Come," I said, with decision, "we will go back; your health is precious. You are rich, respected, admired, beloved; you are happy, as once I was. You are a man to be missed. For me it is no matter. We will go back; you will be ill, and I cannot be responsible. Besides, there is Luchresi—"

"Enough," he said; "the cough is a mere nothing; it will not kill me. I shall not die of a cough."

"True—true," I replied; "and, indeed, I had no intention of alarming you unnecessarily—but you should use all proper caution. A draught of this Medoc[8] will defend us from the damps." Here I knocked off the neck of a bottle which I drew from a long row of its fellows that lay upon the mould. "Drink," I said, presenting him the wine.

He raised it to his lips with a leer. He paused and nodded to me familiarly, while his bells jingled.

"I drink," he said, the buried that repose around us."

"And I to your long life."

He again took my arm, and we proceeded.

"These vaults," he said, "are extensive."

"The Montresors," I replied, "were a great and numerous family. "

"I forget your arms."

"A huge human foot d'or, in a field azure; the foot crushes a serpent rampant whose fangs are imbedded in the heel."

"And the motto?"

"Nemo me impune lacessit.[9]"

"Good!" he said.

The wine sparkled in his eyes and the bells jingled. My own fancy grew warm with the Medoc. We had passed through long walls of piled skeletons, with casks and puncheons intermingling, into the inmost recesses of the catacombs. I paused again, and this time I made bold to seize Fortunato by an arm above the elbow.

"The nitre!" I said; "see, it increases. It hangs like moss upon the vaults. We are below the river's bed. The drops of moisture trickle among the bones. Come, we will go back ere it is too late. Your cough—"

"It is nothing," he said; "let us go on. But first, another draught of the Medoc."

I broke and reached him a flagon of De Grave[10]. He emptied it at a breath. His eyes flashed with a fierce light. He laughed and threw the bottle upwards with a gesticulation I did not understand. I looked at him in surprise. He repeated the movement—a grotesque one.

"You do not comprehend?" he said.

"Not I," I replied.

"Then you are not of the brotherhood."

"How?"

"You are not of the masons."

"Yes, yes," I said; "Yes, yes."

"You? Impossible! A mason?"

"A mason," I replied.

"A sign," he said, "a sign."

"It is this," I answered, producing from beneath the folds of my roquelaire a trowel.

"You jest," he exclaimed, recoiling a few paces. "But let us proceed to the Amontillado."

"Be it so," I said, replacing the tool beneath the cloak and again offering him my arm. He leaned upon it heavily. We continued our rout in search of the Amontillado. We passed through a range of low arches, descended, passed on, and descending again, arrived at a deep crypt, in which the foulness of the air caused our flambeaux rather to glow than flame.

At the most remote end of the crypt there appeared another less spacious. Its walls had been lined with human remains, piled to the vault overhead, in the fashion of the great catacombs of Paris. Three sides of this interior crypt were still ornamented in this manner. From the fourth side the bones had been thrown down, and lay promiscuously upon the earth, forming at one point a mound of some size. Within the wall thus exposed by the displacing of the bones, we perceived a still interior crypt or recess, in depth about four feet, in width three, in height six or seven. It seemed to have been constructed for no especial use within itself, but formed merely the interval between two of the colossal supports of the roof of the catacombs, and was backed by one of their circumscribing walls of solid granite.

It was in vain that Fortunato, uplifting his dull torch, endeavoured to pry into the depth of the recess. Its termination the feeble light did not enable us to see.

"Proceed," I said; "herein is the Amontillado. As for Luchresi—"

"He is an ignoramus[11]," interrupted my friend, as he stepped unsteadily forward, while I followed immediately at his heels. In an instant he had reached the extremity of the niche, and finding his progress arrested by the rock, stood stupidly bewildered. A moment more and I had fettered him to the granite. In its surface were two iron staples, distant from each other about two feet, horizontally. From one of these depended a short chain, from the other a padlock. Throwing the links about his waist, it was but the work of a few seconds to secure it. He was too much astounded to resist. Withdrawing the key I stepped back from the recess. "Pass your hand," I said, "over the wall; you cannot help feeling the nitre. Indeed, it is very damp. Once more let me implore you to return. No? Then I must positively leave you. But I will first render you all the little attentions in my power."

"The Amontillado!" ejaculated my friend, not yet recovered from his astonishment.

"True," I replied; "the Amontillado."

As I said these words I busied myself among the pile of bones of which I have before spoken. Throwing them aside, I soon uncovered a quantity of building stone and mortar. With these materials and with the aid of my trowel, I began vigorously to wall up the entrance of the niche.

I had scarcely laid the first tier of the masonry when I discovered that the intoxication of Fortunato had in great measure worn off. The earliest indication I had of this was a low moaning cry from the depth of the recess. It was not the cry of a drunken man. There was then a long and obstinate silence. I laid the second tier, and the third, and the fourth; and then I heard the furious vibration of the chain. The noise lasted for several minutes, during which, that I might hearken to it with the more satisfaction, I ceased my labours and sat down upon the bones. When at last the clanking subsided, I resumed the trowel, and finished without interruption the fifth, the sixth, and the seventh tier. The wall was now nearly upon a level with my breast. I again paused, and holding the flambeaux over the mason-work, threw a few feeble rays upon the figure within.

A succession of loud and shrill screams, bursting suddenly from the throat of the chained form, seemed to thrust me violently back. For a brief moment I hesitated, I trembled. Unsheathing my rapier, I began to grope with it about the recess; but the thought of an instant reassured me. I placed my hand upon the solid fabric of the catacombs and felt satisfied. I reapproached the wall. I replied to the yells of him who clamoured. I re-echoed, I aided, I surpassed them in volume and in strength. I did this, and the clamourer grew still.

It was now midnight, and my task was drawing to a close. I had completed the eighth, the ninth and the tenth tier. I had finished a portion of the last and the eleventh; there remained but a single stone to be fitted and plastered in. I struggled with its weight; I placed it partially in its destined position. But now there came from out the niche a low laugh that erected the hairs upon my head. It was succeeded by a sad voice, which I had difficulty in recognizing as that of the noble Fortunato. The voice said—

"Ha! ha! ha!—he! he! he!—a very good joke, indeed—an excellent jest. We will have many a rich laugh about it at the palazzo—he! he! he!—over our wine —he! he! he!"

"The Amontilladon!" said.

"He! he! he!—he! he! he!—yes, the Amontillado. But is it not getting late? Will not they be awaiting us at the palazzo—the Lady Fortunato and the rest? Let us be gone."

"Yes," I said, "let us be gone."

"For the love of God, Montresor!"

"Yes," I said, "for the love of God!"

But to these words I hearkened in vain for a reply. I grew impatient. I called aloud—"Fortunato!" No answer. I called again—

"Fortunato!"

No answer still. I thrust a torch through the remaining aperture and let it fall within. There came forth in return only a jingling of the bells. My heart grew sick;

it was the dampness of the catacombs that made it so. I hastened to make an end of my labour. I forced the last stone into its position; I plastered it up. Against the new masonry I re-erected the old rampart of bones. For the half of a century no mortal has disturbed them. In pace requiescat![12]

Question:

1. Who is the narrator? What wrong does he want to redress?
2. What is the pretext he uses to lure Fortunato to his wine cellar?
3. What happens to Fortunato in the end?
4. Describe briefly how Poe characterizes Montresor and Fortunato as contrasts?

注　释

1. I must not only punish but punish with impunity. 我不仅必须要惩罚，而且还要使自己不受伤害地实施惩罚。蒙特利瑟一方面发誓要报复弗图纳多，另一方面还想方设法使报复行为神不知鬼不晓，自己不会因此而受到牵连。
2. quack：冒充内行的人；二五眼；骗子。
3. motley：小丑穿的色彩斑斓的服装。
4. Amontillado：一种低度的西班牙葡萄酒。
5. nitre：硝石。
6. roquelaire：一种可以垂及膝盖的斗篷。
7. palazzo：豪华的宫殿；邸宅。
8. Medoc：产于法国波尔多的一种葡萄酒。
9. Nemo me impune lacessit. 拉丁文，意为：谁也不能侮辱我而不受到惩罚。
10. De Grave：产于法国波尔多的一种白葡萄酒。
11. ignoramus：笨人；毫无知识的人。
12. In pace requiescat! 拉丁语，意为：愿他安息。

第三章
纳撒尼尔·霍桑Nathaniel Hawthorne

作者简介

纳撒尼尔·霍桑（Nathaniel Hawthorne, 1804—1864），小说家。生于没落的殖民官僚家庭，四岁丧父，后由亲戚资助上大学，同学中包括后来闻名的诗人朗费罗以及当选为美国第14届总统的富兰克林·皮尔斯。在大学时代，他开始钟情于文学创作，1825年曾自费出版小说《范肖》(Fanshawe)。毕业后，他一度像隐士一样避免与外界联系，闭门专事写作，作品主要为短篇小说，大多结集收入《故事重述》(Twice-told Tales, 1837）和《古宅青苔》(Mosses from an Old Manse, 1846）。1838年，他结婚后，为了维持家庭生计只好搁置创作，在波士顿海关谋得一份工作。1842年，他迁居拥有众多文化名人居住的康科特，再次开始专心创作，作品多为短篇小说和非虚构性的小品文。40年代末，他开始致力于创作长篇小说，1850年出版其代表作《红字》(The Scarlet Letter)，从而一举成名。随后出版的长篇小说包括《带有七个尖角阁的房子》(The House of the Seven Gables, 1851）、《福谷传奇》(The Blithedale Romance, 1852）和《玉石雕像》(The Marble Faun, 1860）。此外，他还发表了一些儿童读物，并出版了《故事重述》扩容后的版本。皮尔斯当选为总统后于1853年任命霍桑为美国驻英国利物浦的总领事。在完成为期三年的任职后，他侨居意大利，但没有中断创作，在当地写就《玉石雕像》。1864年，他在与皮尔斯一道旅行时去世，遗留下四部尚未完成的长篇小说的残稿。

内容提要

选篇出自《红字》第二章。该小说以17世纪的波士顿为背景。女主人公白兰(Hester Prynne)原本生活在英国，与身体有残疾的科学家齐里沃斯(Ghillingworth)婚后过着平淡无奇的日子，后来按照丈夫的吩咐前往波士顿。齐里沃斯打算随后也赴北美与妻子一道谋生，但因事未能如期成行。白兰与年轻的牧师狄姆斯台尔(Dimmesdale)相识后相爱，以隐秘的方式维系爱情。一年之后，他们的女儿珍珠出生，于是白兰成为众矢之的，被投入监狱，但拒绝说出珍珠生身父亲的姓名。她被判终身在胸前佩戴代表“私通”(Adultery)的红字“A”。在狄姆斯台尔的协助下，白兰得到了抚养珍珠的权利，依靠做针线活维持生计。齐里沃斯来到波士顿后，发誓要找出珍珠的父亲。他没有公开其身份，以行医为业暗中寻访。狄姆斯台尔备受煎熬，身心交瘁，计划与白兰一道出逃，但没有成功。齐里沃斯终于发现了白兰与狄姆斯台尔之间的关系，想方设法折磨狄姆斯台尔。在最后一次布道时，狄姆斯台尔承认他就是珍珠的父亲，随即撕开衣襟，裸露出胸膛上刻有的鲜红字母“A”，然后倒在白兰的怀中停止了呼吸。后来，齐里沃斯也因苦厄沉重而过世，白兰则以其正直、善良的品格以及对于生活的信念重新赢得了社会的承认。珍珠结婚后回到英国定居。白兰去世后，按照她的意愿安葬在狄姆斯台尔的墓旁。

赏　析

作为一部历史题材的小说,《红字》描写了 17世纪北美新英格兰清教社会的生活风貌。但是正如霍桑在小说的序言中所言，他要讲述的故事是具有“符合人的心灵的真实”，而并非刻意追求人物客观经历的绝对真实性。他将这部小说称之为“传奇”，旨在开拓一块“中立的领域”，使“现实”和“想象”的因素可以在此和谐地融为一体。就作品的主题而言，霍桑通过刻画特定的清教环境中的三种罪人，包括犯有“私通”行为的白兰，虚伪的狄姆斯台尔，以及疯狂报复的齐里沃斯，在较深的层次上探讨了清教社会的本质，尤其是人类本性中的善恶与社会环境的关系。

与他同时代的许多作家一样，霍桑也擅长使用象征的手法。在《红字》中，这一创作特征尤为引人注目。白兰被迫在胸前佩戴的红字“A”，与狄姆斯台尔暗自在胸膛上烙刻的“A”一样，是寓意为“私通”的象征性符号，表明他们在道德价值观方面与当时正统清教意识形态的尖锐冲突，以及因为他们的违规行为而必须受到的惩罚。狄姆斯台尔藏匿在胸膛上的红字，一方面表示带有自虐性质的自我惩罚，另一方面也提示他在躲避自己必须承担的责任和义务，掩饰内在的痛苦，从而与他一派岸然而为人爱戴的牧师形象形成具有讽刺意义的反差，衬托出这一人物复杂的个性。特别应当提及的是，小说中某些象征手法的含义呈现出动态演变的特征。例如，由于白兰的人物形象随着故事的演进发生了嬗变，她所佩戴的红字也随之具有了不同的象征意义，由代表“私通”转化为指代“天使”(Angel)和“才干”(Able)。此外，齐里沃斯老迈，身体残疾，不仅在外在形象上与青春、善良的白兰形成鲜明的对比，象征着某种落伍、甚至腐朽的存在，而且他病态的体表特征也是其内在人格缺陷的彰显写照。

小说叙事结构的设计独具匠心。霍桑致力于表现重大冲突发生之后的故事，而并非以故事的自然发展时间为序叙述冲突发生的前因后果。因此，小说一开篇便描写白兰与狄姆斯台尔东窗事发，她与女儿珍珠被囚禁于监狱并面临法庭审判的情形。冲突陡然凸现，不仅加强了故事的张力，而且使这一情境中每个人物的一举一动都更为典型地揭示其个性的本质特征。在故事正文文本之外，小说还附有作为序言的“海关”一文，内容与作品的虚构叙事部分组成一个有机的整体。其中，霍桑大致交代了故事发生时的历史文化背景以及他的小说创作理论和对于社会本质的见解。

The Scarlet Letter

Chapter 2

THE MARKET PLACE

The grass-plot before the jail, in Prison Lane, on a certain summer morning, not less than two centuries ago, was occupied by a pretty large number of the inhabitants of Boston; all with their eyes intently fastened on the iron-clamped oaken door. Amongst any other population, or at a later period in the history of New England, the grim rigidity that petrified the bearded physiognomies of these good people would have augured some awful business in hand. It could have betokened nothing short of the anticipated execution of some noted culprit, on whom the sentence of a legal tribunal had but confirmed the verdict of public sentiment. But, in that early severity of the Puritan character, an inference of this kind could not so indubitably be drawn. It might be that a sluggish bond-servant, or an undutiful child, whom his parents had given over to the civil authority, was to be corrected at the whipping-post. It might be, that an Antinomian[1], a Quaker, or other heterodox religionist, was to be scourged out of the town, or an idle and vagrant Indian, whom the white man's fire-water[2] had made riotous about the streets, was to be driven with stripes into the shadow of the forest. It might be, too, that a witch, like old Mistress Hibbins[3], the bitter-tempered widow of the magistrate, was to die upon the gallows. In either case, there was very much the same solemnity of demeanour on the part of the spectators; as befitted a people amongst whom religion and law were almost identical[4], and in whose character both were so thoroughly interfused, that the mildest and the severest acts of public discipline were alike made venerable and awful. Meagre, indeed, and cold, was the sympathy that a transgressor might look for, from such bystanders at the scaffold. On the other hand, a penalty which, in our days, would infer a degree of mocking infamy and ridicule, might then be invested with almost as stern a dignity as the punishment of death itself.

It was a circumstance to be noted, on the summer morning when our story begins its course, that the women, of whom there were several in the crowd, appeared to take a peculiar interest in whatever penal infliction might be expected to ensue. The age had not so much refinement, that any sense of impropriety restrained the wearers of petticoat and farthingale[5] from stepping forth into the public ways, and wedging their not unsubstantial persons, if occasion were, into the throng nearest to the scaffold at an execution. Morally, as well as materially, there was a coarser fibre in those wives and maidens of old English birth and breeding, than in their fair descendants, separated from them by a series of six or seven generations; for, throughout that chain of ancestry, every successive mother has transmitted to her child a fainter bloom, a more delicate and briefer beauty, and a slighter physical frame, if not a character of less force and solidity, than her own. The women, who were now standing about the prison-door, stood within less than half a century of the period when the man-like Elizabeth[6] had been the not altogether unsuitable representative of the sex. They were her countrywomen; and the beef and ale of their native land, with a moral diet not a whit more refined, entered largely into their composition. The bright morning sun, therefore, shone on broad shoulders and well-developed busts, and on round and ruddy cheeks, that had ripened in the far-off island, and had hardly yet grown paler or thinner in the atmosphere of New England. There was, moreover, a boldness and rotundity of speech among these matrons, as most of them seemed to be, that would startle us at the present day, whether in respect to its purport or its volume of tone.

"Goodwives," said a hard-featured dame of fitly, "I'll tell ye a piece of my mind. It would be greatly for the public behoof[7], if we women, being of mature age and church-members in good repute, should have the handling of such malefactresses as this Hester Prynne. What think ye[8], gossips[9]? If the hussy stood up for judgment before us five, that are now here in a knot together, would she come off with such a sentence as the worshipful magistrates have awarded?

Marry, I trow not![10]"

"People say," said another, "that the Reverend Master Dimmesdale, her godly pastor, takes it very grievously to heart that such a scandal should have come upon his congregation."

"The magistrates are God-fearing gentlemen, but merciful overmuch,—that is a truth, "added a third autumnal matron[11]. "At the very least, they should have put the brand of a hot iron on Hester Prynne's forehead. Madam Hester would have winced at that, I warrant me. But she,—the naughty baggage[12], —little will she care what they put upon the bodice of her gown! Why, look you, she may cover it with a brooch, or such like heathenish adornment, and so walk the streets as brave as ever!"

"Ah, but," interposed, more softly, a young wife, holding a child by the hand, "let her cover the mark as she will, the pang of it will be always in her heart."

"What do we talk of marks and brands, whether on the bodice of her gown, or the flesh of her forehead?" cried another female, the ugliest as well as the most pitiless of these self-constituted judges. "This woman has brought shame upon us all, and ought to die. Is there not law for it? Truly there is, both in the Scripture and the statute-book[13]. Then let the magistrates, who have made it of no effect, thank themselves if their own wives and daughters go astray!"

"Mercy on us, goodwife," exclaimed a man in the crowd, "is there no virtue in woman, save what springs from a wholesome fear of the gallows? That is the hardest word yet! Hush, now, gossips; for the lock is turning in the prison-door, and here comes Mistress Prynne herself."

The door of the jail being flung open from within, there appeared, in the first place, like a black shadow emerging into the sunshine, the grim and grisly presence of the town-beadle, with a sword by his side and his staff of office in his hand. The personage prefigured and represented in his aspect the whole dismal severity of the Puritanic code of law, which it was his business to administer in its final and closest application to the offender. Stretching forth the official staff in his left hand, he laid his right upon the shoulder of a young woman, whom he thus drew forward; until, on the threshold of the prison-door, she repelled him, by an action marked with natural dignity and force of character, and stepped into the open air, as if by her own free-will. She bore in her arms a child, a baby of some three months old, who winked and turned aside its little face from the too vivid light of day; because its existence, heretofore, had brought it acquainted only with the gray twilight of a dungeon, or other darksome apartment of the prison.

When the young woman—the mother of this child—stood fully revealed before the crowd, it seemed to be her first impulse to clasp the infant closely to her bosom; not so much by an impulse of motherly affection, as that she might thereby conceal a certain token, which was wrought or fastened into her dress. In a moment, however, wisely judging that one token of her shame would but poorly serve to hide another, she took the baby on her arm, and, with a burning blush, and yet a haughty smile, and a glance that would not be abashed, looked around at her townspeople and neighbours. On the breast of her gown, in fine red cloth, surrounded with an elaborate embroidery and fantastic flourishes of gold thread, appeared the letter A. It was so artistically done, and with so much fertility and gorgeous luxuriance of fancy, that it had all the effect of a last and fitting decoration to the apparel which she wore; and which was of a splendor in accordance with the taste of the age, but greatly beyond what was allowed by the sumptuary regulations of the colony.

The young woman was tall, with a figure of perfect elegance, on a large scale. She had dark and abundant hair, so glossy that it threw off the sunshine with a gleam, and a face which, besides being beautiful from regularity of feature and richness of complexion, had the impressiveness belonging to a marked brow and deep black eyes. She was lady-like, too, after the manner of the feminine gentility of those days; characterized by a certain state and dignity, rather than by the delicate, evanescent, and indescribable grace, which is now recognized as its indication. And never had Hester Prynne appeared more lady-like, in the antique interpretation of the term, than as she issued from the prison. Those who had before known her, and had expected to behold her dimmed and obscured by a disastrous cloud, were astonished, and even startled, to perceive how her beauty shone out, and made a halo of the misfortune and ignominy in which she was enveloped. It may be true, that, to a sensitive observer, there was something exquisitely painful in it. Her attire, which, indeed, she had wrought for the occasion, in prison, and had modelled much after her own fancy, seemed to express the attitude of her spirit, the desperate recklessness of her mood, by its wild and picturesque peculiarity. But the point which drew all eyes, and, as it were, transfigured the wearer,—so that both men and women, who had been familiarly acquainted with Hester Prynne, were now impressed as if they beheld her for the first time,—was that SCARLET LETTER, so fantastically embroidered and illuminated upon her bosom. It had the effect of a spell[14], taking her out of the ordinary relations with humanity, and inclosing her in a sphere by herself.

"She hath good skill at her needle, that's certain," remarked one of the female spectators; "but did ever a woman, before this brazen hussy, contrive such a way of showing it! Why, gossips, what is it but to laugh in the faces of our godly magistrates, and make a pride out of what they, worthy gentlemen, meant for a punishment?"

"It were well," muttered the most iron-visaged[15] of the old dames, "if we stripped Madam Hester's rich gown off her dainty shoulders; and as for the red letter, which she hath stitched so curiously, I'll bestow a rag of mine own rheumatic flannel[16], to make a fitter one!"

"O, peace, neighbours, peace!" whispered their youngest companion. "Do not let her hear you! Not a stitch in that embroidered letter, but she has felt it in her heart."

The grim beadle now made a gesture with his staff.

"Make way, good people, make way, in the King's name," cried he. "Open a passage; and, I promise ye, Mistress Prynne shall be set where man, woman, and child may have a fair sight of her brave apparel, from this time till an hour past meridian. A blessing on the righteous Colony of the Massachusetts[17], where iniquity is dragged out into the sunshine! Come along, Madam Hester, and show your scarlet letter in the market-place!"

A lane was forthwith opened through the crowd of spectators. Preceded by the beadle, and attended by an irregular procession of stern-browed men and unkindly-visaged women, Hester Prynne set forth towards the place appointed for her punishment. A crowd of eager and curious schoolboys, understanding little of the matter in hand, except that it gave them a half-holiday, ran before her progress, turning their heads continually to stare into her face, and at the winking baby in her arms, and at the ignominious letter on her breast. It was no great distance, in those days, from the prison-door to the market-place. Measured by the prisoner's experience, however, it might be reckoned a journey of some length; for, haughty as her deameanour was, she perchance underwent an agony from every footstep of those that thronged to see her, as if her heart had been flung into the street for them all to spurn and trample upon. In our nature, however, there is a provision, alike marvellous and merciful, that the sufferer should never know the intensity of what he endures by its present torture, but chiefly by the pang that rankles after it. With almost a serene deportment, therefore, Hester Prynne passed through this portion of her ordeal, and came to a sort of scaffold, at the western extremity of the market-place. It stood nearly beneath the eaves of Boston's earliest church, and appeared to be a fixture there.

In fact, this scaffold constituted a portion of a penal machine, which now, for two or three generations past, has been merely historical and traditionary among us, but was held, in the old time, to be as effectual an agent in the promotion of good citizenship, as ever was the guillotine among the terrorists of France[18]. It was, in short, the platform of the pillory; and above it rose the framework of that instrument of discipline, so fashioned as to confine the human head in its tight grasp, and thus hold it up to the public gaze. The very ideal of ignominy was embodied and made manifest in this contrivance of wood and iron. There can be no outrage, methinks, against our common nature,—whatever be the delinquencies of the individual,—no outrage more flagrant than to forbid the culprit to hide his face for shame; as it was the essence of this punishment to do. In Hester Prynne's instance, however, as not unfrequently in other cases, her sentence bore, that she should stand a certain time upon the platform, but without undergoing that gripe about the neck and confinement of the head, the proneness to which was the most devilish characteristic of this ugly engine. Knowing well her part, she ascended a flight of wooden steps, and was thus displayed to the surrounding multitude, at about the height of a man's shoulders above the street.

Had there been a Papist[19] among the crowd of Puritans, he might have seen in this beautiful woman, so picturesque in her attire and mien, and with the infant at her bosom, an object to remind him of the image of Divine Maternity[20], which so many illustrious painters have vied with one another to represent; something which should remind him, indeed, but only by contrast, of that sacred image of sinless motherhood[21], whose infant was to redeem the world. Here, there was the taint of deepest sin in the most sacred quality of human life, working such effect, that the world was only the darker for this woman's beauty, and the more lost for the infant that she had borne.

The scene was not without a mixture of awe, such as must always invest the spectacle of guilt and shame in a fellow-creature, before society shall have grown corrupt enough to smile, instead of shuddering at it. The witnesses of Hester Prynne's disgrace had not yet passed beyond their simplicity. They were stern enough to look upon her death, had that been the sentence, without a murmur at its severity, but had none of the heartlessness of another social state, which would find only a theme for jest in an exhibition like the present. Even had there been a disposition to turn the matter into ridicule, it must have been repressed and overpowered by the solemn presence of men no less dignified than the Governor, and several of his counsellors, a judge, a general, and the ministers of the town; all of whom sat or stood in a balcony of the meeting-house, looking down upon the platform. When such personages could constitute a part of the spectacle, without risking the majesty or reverence of rank and office, it was safely to be inferred that the infliction of a legal sentence would have an earnest and effectual meaning. Accordingly, the crowd was sombre and grave. The unhappy culprit sustained herself as best a woman might, under the heavy weight of a thousand unrelenting eyes, all fastened upon her, and concentred at her bosom. It was almost intolerable to be borne. Of an impulsive and passionate nature, she had fortified herself to encounter the stings and venomous stabs of public contumely, wreaking itself in every variety of insult; but there was a quality so much more terrible in the solemn mood of the popular mind, that she longed rather to behold all those rigid countenances contorted with scornful merriment, and herself the object. Had a roar of laughter burst from the multitude,—each man, each woman, each little shrill-voiced child, contributing their individual parts,—Hester Prynne might have repaid them all with a bitter and disdainful smile. But, under the leaden infliction which it was her doom to endure, she felt, at moments, as if she must needs shriek out with the full power of her lungs, and cast herself from the scaffold down upon the ground, or else go mad at once.

Yet there were intervals when the whole scene, in which she was the most conspicuous object, seemed to vanish from her eyes, or, at least, glimmered indistinctly before them, like a mass of imperfectly shaped and spectral images. Her mind, and especially her memory, was preternaturally active, and kept bringing up other scenes than this roughly hewn street of a little town, on the edge of the Western wilderness[22]; other faces than were lowering upon her from beneath the brims of those steeple-crowned hats. Reminiscences, the most trifling and immaterial, passages of infancy and school-days, sports, childish quarrels, and the little domestic traits of her maiden years, came swarming back upon her, intermingled with recollections of whatever was gravest in her subsequent life; one picture precisely as vivid as another; as if all were of similar importance, or all alike a play. Possibly, it was an instinctive device of her spirit, to relieve itself, by the exhibition of these phantasmagoric forms, from the cruel weight and hardness of the reality.

Be that as it might, the scaffold of the pillory was a point of view that revealed to Hester Prynne the entire track along which she had been treading; since her happy infancy. Standing on that miserable eminence, she saw again her native village, in Old England[23], and her paternal home; a decayed house of gray stone, with a poverty-stricken aspect, but retaining a half-obliterated shield of arms over the portal, in token of antique gentility. She saw her father's face, with its bald brow, and reverend white beard, that flowed over the old-fashioned Elizabethan' ruff[25]; her mother's, too, with the look of heedful and anxious love which it always wore in her remembrance, and which, even since her death, had so often laid the impediment of a gentle remonstrance in her daughter's pathway. She saw her own face, glowing with girlish beauty, and illuminating all the interior of the dusky mirror in which she had been wont to gaze at it. There she beheld another countenance, of a man well stricken in years, a pale, thin, scholar-like visage, with eyes dim and bleared by the lamp-light that had served them to pore over many ponderous books. Yet those same bleared optics had a strange, penetrating power, when it was their owner's purpose to read the human soul. This figure of the study and the cloister, as Hester Prynne's womanly fancy failed not to recall, was slightly deformed, with the left shoulder a trifle higher than the right. Next rose before her, in memory's picture-gallery, the intricate and narrow thoroughfares, the tall, gray houses, the huge cathedrals, and the public edifices, ancient in date and quaint in architecture, of a Continental city[25], where a new life had awaited her, still in connection with the misshapen scholar[26]; a new life, but feeding itself on time-worn materials, like a tuft of green moss on a crumbling wall. Lastly, in lieu of these shilling scenes, came back the rude market-place of the Puritan settlement, with all the townspeople assembled and levelling their stern regards at Hester Prynne,—yes, at herself,—who stood on the scaffold of the pillory, an infant on her arm, and the letter A, in scarlet, fantastically embroidered with gold thread, upon her bosom!

Could it be true? She clutched the child so fiercely to her breast, that it sent forth a cry; she turned her eyes downward at the scarlet letter, and even touched it with her finger, to assure herself that the infant and the shame were real. Yes!—these were her realities, —all else had vanished!

Questions:

1. Why is the prison the setting of Chapter I and what is the implication of the description of the roses?
2. Describe the appearance of Hester Prynne and the attitude of the people towards her.
3. What has happened to Hester? Why does she make the embroidery of the letter A so elaborate? How does this tell us about her character?

注　释

1. Antinomian：唯信仰论者；道德律废弃论者。其主要信条是，基督徒只是恪守《圣经》中的道德法律，无济于事，只有坚信上帝无所不知，无所不能，才能使自己的灵魂得到拯救。
2. fire-water：烈酒。

3. Old Mistress Hibbins：指真实的历史人物Ann Hibbins。1655年，她因被指控使用巫术而受审，1656年被处以绞刑。
4. ...religion and law were almost identical...意为“宗教和法律几乎完全相同”，指17世纪北美殖民时期清教占统治地位时政教合一的神权政治。
5. farthingale：即蓬裙（hoopskirt），有裙环的女裙。
6. the man-like Elizabeth：指英国女王伊丽莎白一世（Queen Elizabeth I），在位期间为1558年至1603年，治国安邦，建树非凡，其管理社稷的才干不亚于男性君主，所以小说的叙事者称赞她具有男子气概。
7. ye：你们，在古英语中是“你”（thou）的复数形式。
8. behoof：利益，常见于古英语中，相当于benefit。
9. gossips：（女性）朋友或者同伴。
10. Mary, I trow not! Mary指圣母玛丽亚（Virgin Mary），此处用作感叹词，表示惊讶；trow意为think，或者suppose。
11. autumnal matron：年过半百的已婚妇人。
12. the naughty baggage：意为“坏女人”，骂有性违规行为的女人的词语。
13. the Scripture and the statute-book：指《圣经》和法令全书。《圣经·旧约》中有处死犯有通奸罪的男女的条文。
14. spell：符咒，咒语。
15. iron-visaged：铁面无情的。
16. a rag of mine own rheumatic flannel：我患风湿病时用过的一块法兰绒；在古英语中，mine意为my。
17. the Colony of the Massachusetts：马萨诸塞殖民地，是后来组成美利坚合众国的最早的13个殖民地之一，首府即故事发生的地点波士顿。
18. the terrorists of France：法国的恐怖分子，指法国资产阶级革命过程中雅各宾派曾于1793年至1794年采取的恐怖政策。
19. Papist：罗马天主教徒（含贬义）。
20. the image of Divine Maternity：指圣母玛丽亚的形象。
21. sinless motherhood：指圣母玛丽亚接受圣灵而孕育耶稣。

22. the Western wilderness：指美国的西部。欧洲移民初到北美时，是在东海岸建立殖民地，尔后才逐步向西部开发。
23. Old England：指英国。英国移民初到北美时，常以本国的某些地名命名北美的殖民地，但在原有的地名前加上New，以示区别，例如 New England, New York, New Hampshire。
24. Elizabethan ruff：指做工精美而且坚硬的衣领，流行于16、17世纪英国的上流社会。
25. a Continental city：指阿姆斯特丹。英国的许多清教徒在移民北美之前需在阿姆斯特丹逗留，等待许可证。
26. the misshapen scholar：即白兰的丈夫齐里沃斯。

第四章
赫尔曼·梅尔维尔Herman Melville

作者简介

赫尔曼·梅尔维尔（Herman Melville, 1819—1891），小说家，诗人。生于商人家庭，11岁父亲亡故，家道中落。15岁辍学后，他自谋生计，先后充当银行职员、文书、店员、农场工人和教师，生活飘泊不定。自1839年起，他出海谋生，在各种轮船上任侍者和水手，航海的经历为他的文学创作积累了厚实的素材。1866年至1885年，他曾任纽约海关官员，1891年因病而逝。19世纪40年代初，他着手写作小说，1846年发表《泰比》（Typee），次年又发表了《欧穆》（Omoo），以游记体的叙事风格讲述南太平洋一个小岛上土著人的生活。此后，他同样以航海生活为背景创作了一系列更为成熟的小说，包括《玛地》（Mardi, 1849）、《雷得本》（Rectourn, 1849）、《白外衣》（White Jacket, 1850）、《白鲸》（Moby Dick, 1851）以及《骗子的化装表演》（The Confidence Man, 1857）。但他在世时，批评界对他的小说的反应较为冷淡，贬甚于褒。19世纪60年代后期，他创作小说的热情逐渐消退，转而致力于写诗。1866年自费出版其首部诗集《战事集》（Battle Pieces），以美国内战为主题。在此后的20余年中，他不仅自费刊印了长诗《克拉瑞尔》（Clarel, 1876），还出资出版了《约翰·玛尔和其他水手》（John Marr and Other Sailors, 1888）与《梯摩里昂》（Timoieon, 1891）等两部诗集，然而如同他的小说一样，始终没有引起阅读大众和批评界的注意。临终前，他完成了最后一部长篇小说《毕利·伯德》（Billy Budd），但未及出版。这部小说后来于1924年出版。

内容提要

“皮阔德”号捕鲸船的船长名叫埃哈伯，他以捕鲸为业，航海40余年。一次在与一群鲸鱼搏斗时，他不慎被一条凶猛的白色鲸鱼咬掉了一条腿。这条鲸鱼因躯体庞大、性情刁钻凶虐而闻名，水手们称它为莫比·狄克。埃哈伯决计不惜一切代价找到莫比·狄克，报仇雪恨。他的心愿得到了全体船员的理解和支持，大家饮酒发誓，决定再次出海捕杀莫比·狄克。他率领全体船员长途航行，途经南太平洋和印度洋，历尽艰险，终于来到了莫比·狄克频繁出没的日本海。途中，“皮阔德”号遇到数艘返航的捕鲸船，对方不仅告诉埃哈伯及其船员白鲸逞凶所造成的新的伤害，而且忠言相劝，希望他们放弃捕杀白鲸的计划，但无济于事。埃哈伯要求船员继续前行，尽管风暴已经给船只造成了严重损坏。“皮阔德”号与白鲸相遇后，彼此殊死搏斗了3天，最后埃哈伯用尽全身的气力将鱼叉刺进白鲸的腹部，这致命的一击最终结束了白鲸的生命。但由于鱼叉末端的绳索缠绕在埃哈伯的颈部，所以白鲸在垂死挣扎时,不仅将他带入大海中殒命，而且将“皮阔德”号的船头撞碎，全体船员坠海丧生,只有以实玛利被另一艘捕鲸船搭救。作为唯一的幸存者，他生还后讲述了上述故事。

选篇出自《白鲸》第41章。在这章里，以实玛利跟大家一样，支持埃哈伯捕杀莫比·狄克。他接着介绍了有关这条鲸鱼的一些传说。

赏　析

《白鲸》是一部社会生活内涵和艺术内涵都相当丰富的小说。从写实的层面来看，梅尔维尔以自己的航海生活和捕鲸经历为基础并参阅了大量的捕鲸文献，用真实而生动的笔触描写了19世纪北美渔业捕鲸船员的生活。小说全面而细腻地描述了捕鲸船员追捕鲸鱼和提炼鲸油的过程，诸如如何寻找鲸鱼，识别它们的类别，了解它们的生活习性，如何以最小的代价捕捉它们并最大限度地提炼鲸油，堪称一部百科全书式的捕鲸著作。此外，作品还再现了捕鲸船员乐观、勇敢、坚韧、豪爽的品格和他们的生活方式。就社会观而言，梅尔维尔塑造的人物具有较为典型的价值和意义。捕鲸船员在捕杀性情暴烈、凶悍的鲸鱼的过程中所表现的征服欲望，不只是从事捕鲸业的人们特有的品性，实际上也是他们所处时代的精神写照。

小说的价值还在于作者对于人类命运以及人类与外在世界的关系的思考。在这一点上，梅尔维尔与同时代的小说家霍桑一样，尤为关注人性中局部的缺陷,或者某一方面的邪恶对其整个命运的影响。埃哈伯偏执、自私的性格缺陷，不仅导致他自己在疯狂的复仇过程中丧生，而且也连累全体船员作为牺牲品葬身海洋，使作为大自然的缩影的白鲸也付出了生命的代价。

在艺术技巧方面，象征手法在作品中发挥了重要作用。在梅尔维尔的视野中，捕鲸船员以及他们的船长埃哈伯是全人类的化身，偏执和盲从是其致命的弱点。白鲸莫比·狄克作为小说中的核心形象，也载荷着重要而复杂的象征意义。一般认为，它作为与人产生矛盾的对立面，代表大自然中神秘莫测而且不可征服的规 律。然而它巨大的身躯所拥有的白色，也象征着人性和自然中纯真的特性。以实玛利是小说中第一人称的叙事者，他的名字取自《圣经》，意为被逐出的人。但作为船员中唯一的幸存者，他得到了命运的关照，从丧生的船员群体中脱身而出。这种结局一则验证了以实玛利作为人物名字的寓意，再则也是在启发读者思考这 个人物之所以能够得以幸存的非偶然因素。简而言之，在梅尔维尔的心目中，以实玛利区别与他人之处，主要在于他的知识修养、对于未知事物的自觉探索以及审时度势的处世方式。

Moby Dick

Chapter 41

I, ISHMAEL[1], was one of that crew; my shouts had gone up with the rest; my oath had been welded with theirs; and stronger I shouted, and more did I hammer and clinch my oath, because of the dread in my soul. A wild, mystical, sympathetical feeling was in me; Ahab's[2] quenchless feud seemed mine. With greedy ears I learned the history of that murderous monster against whom I and all the others had taken our oaths of violence and revenge.

For some time past, though at intervals only, the unaccompanied, secluded White Whale[3] had haunted those uncivilized seas mostly frequented by the Sperm Whale[4] fishermen. But not all of them knew of his existence; only a few of them, comparatively, had knowingly seen him; while the number who as yet had actually and knowingly given battle to him, was small indeed. For, owing to the large number of whale-cruisers; the disorderly way they were sprinkled over the entire watery circumference, many of them adventurously pushing their quest along solitary latitudes, so as seldom or never for a whole twelvemonth or more on a stretch, to encounter a single news- telling sail of any sort; the inordinate length of each separate voyage; the irregularity of the times of sailing from home; all these, with other circumstances, direct and indirect, long obstructed the spread through the whole world-wide whaling-fleet of the special individualizing tidings concerning Moby Dick[5]. It was hardly to be doubted, that several vessels reported to have encountered, at such or such a time, or on such or such a meridian, a Sperm Whale of uncommon magnitude and malignity, which whale, after doing great mischief to his assailants, had completely escaped them; to some minds it was not an unfair presumption, I say, that the whale in question must have been no other than Moby Dick. Yet as of late the Sperm Whale fishery had been marked by various and not unfrequent instances of great ferocity, cunning, and malice in the monster attacked; therefore it was, that those who by accident ignorantly gave battle to Moby Dick; such bunters, perhaps, for the most part, were content to ascribe the peculiar terror he bred, more, as it were, to the perils of the Sperm Whale fishery at large, than to the individual cause. In that way, mostly, the disastrous encounter between Ahab and the whale had hitherto been popularly regarded.

And as for those who, previously hearing of the White Whale, by chance caught sight of him; in the beginning of the thing they had every one of them, almost, as boldly and fearlessly lowered for him, as for any other whale of that species. But at length, such calamities did ensue in these assaults—not restricted to sprained wrists and ankles, broken limbs, or devouring amputations—but fatal to the last degree of fatality; those repeated disastrous repulses, all accumulating and piling their terrors upon Moby Dick; those things had gone far to shake the fortitude of many brave hunters, to whom the story of the White Whale had eventually come.

Nor did wild rumors of all sons fail to exaggerate, and still the more horrify the tale histories of these deadly encounters. For not only do fabulous rumors naturally grow out of the very body of all surprising terrible events,—as the smitten tree gives birth to its fungi; but, in maritime life, far more than in that of *terra firma*[6], wild rumors abound, wherever there is any adequate reality for them to cling to. And as the sea surpasses the land in this matter, so the whale fishery surpasses every other sort of maritime life, in the wonderfulness and fearfulness of the rumors which sometimes circulate there. For not only are whalemen as a body unexempt from that ignorance and superstitiousness hereditary to all sailors; but of all sailors, they are by all odds the most directly brought into contact with whatever is appallingly astonishing in the sea; face to face they not only eye its greatest marvels, but, hand to jaw[7], give battle to them. Alone, in such remotest waters, that though you sailed a thousand miles, and passed a thousand shores, you would not come to any chiselled hearthstone, or aught hospitable, beneath that part of the sun; in such latitudes and longitudes, pursuing too such a calling as he does, the whaleman is wrapped by influences all tending to make his fancy pregnant with many a mighty birth.

No wonder, then, that ever gathering volume from the mere transit over the widest watery spaces, the outblown rumors of the White Whale did in the end incorporate with themselves all manner of morbid hints, and half-formed foetal suggestions of supernatural agencies, which eventually invested Moby Dick with new terrors unborrowed from anything that visibly appears. So that in many cases such a panic did he finally strike, that few who by those rumors, at least, had heard of the White Whale, few of those hunters were willing to encounter the perils of his jaw.

But there were still other and more vital practical influences at work. Not even at the present day has the original prestige of the Sperm Whale, as fearfully distinguished from all other species of the Leviathan[8], died out of the minds of the whalemen as a body. There are those this day among them, who, though intelligent and courageous enough in offering battle to the Greenland or Right Whale[9], would perhaps—either from professional inexperience, or incompetency, or timidity, decline a contest with the Sperm Whale; at any rate, there are plenty of whalemen, especially among those whaling nations not sailing under the American flag, who have never hostilely encountered the Sperm Whale, but whose sole knowledge of the Leviathan is restricted to the ignoble monster primitively pursued in the North; seated on their hatches, these men will hearken with a childish fire-side interest and awe, to the wild, strange tales of Southern whaling. Nor is the pre-eminent tremendousness of the great Sperm Whale anywhere more feelingly comprehended, than on board of those prows which stem him.

And as if the now tested reality of his might had in former legendary times thrown its shadow before it; we find some book naturalists—Olassen and Povelson[10]—declaring the Sperm Whale not only to be a consternation to every other creature in the sea, but also to be so incredibly ferocious as continually to be athirst, for human blood. Nor even down to so late a time as Cuvier's[11] were these or almost similar impressions effaced. For in his Natural History, the Baron[12] himself affirms that at sight of the Sperm Whale, all fish (sharks included) are "struck with the most lively terrors," and "often in the precipitancy of their flight dash themselves against the rocks with such violence as to cause instantaneous death." And however the general experiences in the fishery may amend such reports as these; yet in their full terribleness, even the bloodthirsty item of Povelson, the superstitious belief in them is, in some vicissitudes of their vocation, revived in the minds of the hunters.

So that overawed by the rumors and portents concerning him, not a few of the fishermen recalled, in reference to *Moby Dick*, the earlier days of the Sperm Whale fishery, when it was often-times hard to induce long practised Right Whalemen to embark in the perils of this new and daring warfare; such men protesting that although other Leviathans might be hopefully pursued, yet to chase and point lance at such an apparition as the Sperm Whale was not for mortal man. That to attempt it, would be inevitably to be torn into a quick eternity[13]. On this head, there are some remarkable documents that may be consulted.

Nevertheless, some there were, who even in the face of these things were ready to give chase to Moby Dick; and a still greater number who, chancing only to hear of him distantly and vaguely, without the specific details of any certain calamity, and without superstitious accompaniments, were sufficiently hardy not to flee from the battle if offered.

One of the wild suggestions referred to, as at last coming to be linked with the White Whale in the minds of the superstitiously inclined, was the unearthly conceit that Moby Dick was ubiquitous; that he had actually been encountered in opposite latitudes at one and the same instant of time.

Nor, credulous as such minds must have been, was this conceit altogether without some faint show of superstitious probability. For as the secrets of the currents in the seas have never yet been divulged, even to the most erudite research; so the hidden ways of the Sperm Whale when beneath the surface remain, in great part, unaccountable to his pursuers; and from time to time have originated the most curious and contradictory speculations regarding them, especially concerning the mystic modes whereby, after sounding to a great depth, he transports himself with such vast swiftness to the most widely distant points.

It is a thing well known to both American and English whaleships, and as well a thing placed upon authoritative record years ago by Scoresby[14], that some whales have been captured far north in the Pacific, in whose bodies have been found the barbs of harpoons darted in the Greenland seas. Nor is it to be gainsaid, that in some of these instances it has been declared that the interval of time between the two assaults could not have exceeded very many days. Hence, by inference, it has been believed by some whalemen, that the Nor' West Passage[15], so long a problem to man, was never a problem to the whale. So that here, in the real living experience of living men, the prodigies related in old times of the inland Strello mountain in Portugal (near whose top there was said to be a lake in which the wrecks of ships floated up to the surface); and that still more wonderful story of the Arethusa fountain near Syracuse[16] (whose waters were believed to have come from the Holy Land[17] by an underground passage); these fabulous narrations are almost fully equalled by the realities of the whaleman.

Forced into familiarity, then, with such prodigies as these; and knowing that after repeated, intrepid assaults, the White Whale had escaped alive; it cannot be much matter of surprise that some whalemen should go still further in their superstitions; declaring Moby Dick not only ubiquitous, but immortal (for immortality is but ubiquity in time); that though groves of spears should be planted in his flanks, he would still swim away unharmed; or if indeed he should ever be made to spout thick blood, such a sight would be but a ghastly deception; for again in unensanguined billows hundreds of leagues away, his unsullied jet would once more be seen.

But even stripped of these supernatural surmisings, there was enough in the earthly make and incontestable character of the monster to strike the imagination with unwonted power. For, it was not so much his uncommon bulk that so much distinguished him from other Sperm Whales, but, as was elsewhere thrown out—

a peculiar snow-white wrinkled forehead, and a high, pyramidical white hump. These were his prominent features; the tokens whereby, even in the limitless, uncharted seas, he revealed his identity, at a long distance, to those who knew him.

The rest of his body was so streaked, and spotted, and marbled with the same shrouded hue, that, in the end, he had gained his distinctive appellation of the White Whale; a name, indeed, literally justified by his vivid aspect, when seen gliding at high noon through a dark blue sea, leaving a milky-way wake of creamy foam, all spangled with golden gleamings.

Nor was it his unwonted magnitude, nor his remarkable hue, nor yet his deformed lower jaw, that so much invested the whale with natural terror, as that unexampled, intelligent malignity which, according to specific accounts, he had over and over again evinced in his assaults. More than all, his treacherous retreats struck more of dismay than perhaps aught else. For, when swimming before his exulting pursuers, with every apparent symptom of alarm, he had several times been known to turn round suddenly, and, bearing down upon them, either stave their boats to splinters, or drive them back in consternation to their ship. Already several fatalities had attended his chase. But though similar disasters, however little bruited ashore, were by no means unusual in the fishery; yet, in most instances, such seemed the White Whale's infernal aforethought of ferocity, that every dismembering or death that he caused, was not wholly regarded as having been inflicted by an unintelligent agent.

Judge, then, to what pitches of inflamed, distracted fury the minds of his more desperate hunters were impelled, when amid the chips of chewed boats, and the sinking limbs of torn comrades, they swam out of the white curds of the whale's direful wrath into the serene, exasperating sunlight, that smiled on, as if at a birth or a bridal.

His three boats stove around him, and oars and men both whirling in the eddies; one captain, seizing the line-knife from his broken prow, had dashed at the whale, as an Arkansas duellist at his foe, blindly seeking with a six inch blade to reach the fathom-deep life of the whale. That captain was Ahab. And then it was, that suddenly sweeping his sickle-shaped lower jaw beneath him, Moby Dick had reaped away Ahab's leg, as a mower a blade of grass in the field. No turbaned Turk, no hired Venetian or Malay, could have smote him with more seeming malice. Small reason was there to doubt, then, that ever since that almost fatal encounter, Ahab had cherished a wild vindictiveness against the whale, all the more fell for that in his frantic morbidness he at last came to identify with him, not only all his bodily woes, but all his intellectual and spiritual exasperations. The White Whale swam before him is the monomaniac incarnation of all those malicious agencies which some deep men feel eating in them, till they are left living on with half a heart and half a lung. That intangible malignity which has been from the beginning; to whose dominion even the modem Christians ascribe one-half of the worlds; which the ancient Ophites[18] of the east reverenced in their statue devil; —Ahab did not fall down and worship it like them; but deliriously transferring its idea to the abhorred White Whale, he pitted himself, all mutilated, against it. All that most maddens and torments; all that stirs up the lees of things; all truth with malice in it; all that cracks the sinews and cakes the brain; all the subtle demonisms of life and thought; all evil, to crazy Ahab, were visibly personified, and made practically assailable in Moby Dick. He piled upon the whale's white hump the sum of all the general rage and hate felt by his whole race from Adam down[19]; and then, as if his chest had been a mortar, he burst his hot heart's shell upon it.

It is not probable that this monomania in him took its instant rise at the precise time of his bodily dismemberment. Then, in darting at the monster, knife in hand, he had but given loose to a sudden, passionate, corporal animosity; and when he received the stroke that tore him, he probably but felt the agonizing bodily laceration, but nothing more. Yet, when by this collision forced to turn towards home, and for long months of days and weeks, Ahab and anguish lay stretched together in one hammock, rounding in mid winter that dreary, howling Patagonian Cape[20]; then it was, that his torn body and gashed soul bled into one another; and so interfusing, made him mad. That it was only then, on the homeward voyage, after the encounter, that the final monomania seized him, seems all but certain from the fact that, at intervals during the passage, he was a raving lunatic; and though unlimbed of a leg, yet such vital strength yet lurked in his Egyptian chest[21], and was moreover intensified by his delirium, that his mates were forced to lace him fast, even there, as he sailed, raving in his hammock. In a strait-jacket, he swung to the mad rockings of the gales. And, when running into more sufferable latitudes, the ship, with mild stun' sails[22] spread, floated across the tranquil tropics, and, to all appearances, the old man's delirium seemed left behind him with the Cape Horn[23] swells, and he came forth from his dark den into the blessed light and air; even then, when he bore that firm, collected front, however pale, and issued his calm orders once again; and his mates thanked God the direful madness was now gone; even then, Ahab, in his hidden self, raved on. Human madness is oftentimes a cunning and most feline thing. When you think it fled, it may have but become transfigured into some still subtler form. Ahab's full lunacy subsided not, but deepeningly contracted; like the unabated Hudson[24], when that noble Northman flows narrowly, but unfathomably through the Highland gorge. But, as in his narrow-flowing monomania, not one jot of Ahab's broad madness had been left behind; so in that broad madness, not one jot of his great natural intellect had perished. That before living agent, now became the living instrument. If such a furious trope may stand, his special lunacy stormed his general sanity, and carried it, and turned all its concentrated cannon upon its own mad mark; so that far from having lost his strength, Ahab, to that one end, did now possess a thousand fold more potency than ever he had sanely brought to bear upon any one reasonable object.

This is much; yet Ahab's larger, darker, deeper part remains unhinted. But vain to popularize profundities, and all truth is profound. Winding far down from within the very heart of this spiked Hotel de Cluny[25] where we here stand—however grand and wonderful, now quit it;—and take your way, ye nobler, sadder souls, to those vast Roman halls of Thermes; where far beneath the fantastic towers of man's upper earth, his root of grandeur, his whole awful essence sits in bearded state; an antique buried beneath antiquities, and throned on torsoes! So with a broken throne, the great gods mock that captive king; so like a Caryatid[26], he patient sits, upholding on his frozen brow the piled entablatures of ages. Wind ye down there, ye prouder, sadder souls! question that proud, sad king! A family likeness! Aye, he did beget ye, ye young exiled royalties; and from your grim sire only will the old State-secret come.

Now, in his heart, Ahab had some glimpse of thin, namely: all my means are sane, my motive and my object mad. Yet without power to kill, or change, or shun the fact; he likewise knew that to mankind he did long dissemble; in some sort, did still. But that thing of his dissembling was only subject to his perceptibility, not to his will determinate. Nevertheless, so well did he succeed in that dissembling, that when with ivory leg he stepped ashore at last, no Nantucketer[27] thought him otherwise than but naturally grieved, and that to the quick, with the terrible casualty which had overtaken him.

The report of his undeniable delirium at sea was likewise popularly ascribed to a kindred cause. And so too, all the added moodiness which always afterwards, to the very day of sailing in the Pequod[28] on the present voyage, sat brooding on his brow. Nor is it so very unlikely, that far from distrusting his fitness for another whaling voyage, on account of such dark symptoms, the calculating people of that prudent isle[29] were inclined to harbor the conceit, that for those very reasons he was all the better qualified and set on edge, for a pursuit so full of rage and wildness as the bloody hunt of whales. Gnawed within and scorched without, with the infixed, unrelenting fangs of some incurable idea; such an one, could he be found, would seem the very man to dart his iron and lift his lance against the most appalling of all brutes. Or, if for any reason thought to be corporeally incapacitated for that, yet such an one would seem superlatively competent to cheer and howl on his underlings to the attack. But be all this as it may, certain it is, that with the mad secret of his unabated rage bolted up and keyed in him, Ahab had purposely sailed upon the present voyage with the one only and all-engrossing object of hunting the White Whale. Had any one of his old acquaintances on shore but half dreamed of what was lurking in him then, how soon would their aghast and righteous souls have wrenched the ship from such a fiendish man! They were bent on profitable cruises, the profit to be counted down in dollars from the mint. He was intent on an audacious, immitigable, and supernatural revenge.

Here, then, was this grey-headed, ungodly old man, chasing with curses a Job's whale[30] round the world, at the head of a crew, too, chiefly made up of mongrel renegades, and castaways, and cannibals—morally enfeebled also, by the incompetence of mere unaided virtue or right- mindedness in Starbuck, the invulnerable jollity of indifference and recklessness in Stubb, and the pervading mediocrity in Flask. Such a crew, so officered, seemed specially picked and packed by some infernal fatality to help him to his monomaniac revenge. How it was that they so aboundingly responded to the old man's ire—by what evil magic their souls were possessed, that at times his hate seemed almost theirs; the White Whale as much their insufferable foe as his; how all this came to be—what the White Whale was to them, or how to their unconscious understandings, also, in some dim, unsuspected way, he might have seemed the gliding great demon of the seas of life,—all this to explain, would be to dive deeper than Ishmael can go. The subterranean miner that works in us all, how can one tell whither leads his shaft by the ever shifting, muffled sound of his pick? Who does not feel the irresistible arm drag? What skiff in tow of a seventy-four[31] can stand still? For one, I gave myself up to the abandonment of the time and the place; but while yet all a-rush to encounter the whale, could see naught in that brute but the deadliest ill.

Questions:

1. What are the stories Ismael tells about Moby Dick?
2. Why does Ahab react so violently against the white whale? Ishmael suggests that Ahab is "crazy" and calls him "a raving lunatic." Do you agree with him? Why or why not?
3. What narrative features can you find in the selected chapter?

注 释

1. Ishmael：以实玛利，小说中的叙述者，其姓名源于《圣经》。作为《圣经》中的人物，以实玛利系亚伯拉罕之子，但身为庶出，其母是一女仆。以实玛利后与母亲一道被亚伯拉罕逐出家门。此名字常象征"被遗弃的人"。
2. Ahab：即船长埃哈伯。其姓名也源于《圣经》。在《圣经》里，他是一个极有野心的以色列国王。他遭到老百姓的反对，因为他娶一位异族女子为妻，并不顾民意允许她祭祀她的神祖。但埃哈伯还是一个十分勇敢的人，在战斗中他总是身先士卒，英勇顽强，最后在与叙利亚的战争中英勇牺牲。
3. White Whale：指小说中名为莫比·狄克的白鲸。
4. the Sperm Whale：巨头鲸。
5. Moby Dick：见注3。
6. terra firma：[拉丁语]大陆，陆地。
7. hand to jaw：指人与鲸鱼的斗争，意为船员手持工具与鲸鱼的嘴搏斗。
8. Leviathan：海中怪兽，语出《圣经·旧约》，象征邪恶。
9. Greeland or Right Whale：北极露脊鲸。
10. Olafsen and Povelson：前者为18世纪冰岛生物学家，旅游经历甚多，并有游记出版。后者生平不详。

11. Cuvier：指居维叶（Georges Cuvier, 1769—1832），法国动物学家，以创立比较解剖学和古生物学而闻名。
12. the Baron：即居维叶，他拥有世袭的男爵爵位。参见注11。
13. to be torn into a quick eternity：意为身体被扯烂并旋即毙命。
14. Scoresby：指斯科斯比（William Scoresby, Jr., 1789—1857），英国探险家、科学家、牧师，作为北极科学研究的先驱者而闻名。
15. the Nor' West Passage：沿着加拿大或者美国阿拉斯加州的北冰洋而行并连接大西洋与太平洋的航线。
16. the Arethusa foundation near Syracuse：Arethusa是希腊神话中的一个仙女，她为了躲避河神（Alpheus）的求爱，在Syracuse附近将自己变为小溪。
17. the Holy Land：圣地，即耶稣的故乡巴勒斯坦。
18. the ancient Ophites：蛇派信徒。公元二世纪以及其后几个世纪盛行于罗马帝国的诺斯替教几个派别的成员。他们认为物质（恶）与精神（永恒之神）互相斗争，并以此解释基督教的基本教义。
19. from Adam down：指自从有了人类的祖先亚当以来。
20. Patagonian Cape：指位于南美洲的巴塔哥尼亚海角。
21. in his Egyptian chest：意为"在他拥有的吉普赛人的心胸中"；相传吉普赛人曾长期定居埃及，所以在古英语中，Egyptian通指"埃及人"、"埃及语"、"吉普赛人"和"吉普赛语"。
22. stun' sails：悬挂在主帆侧面的副帆。
23. the Cape Horn：位于智利的合恩角。
24. the unabated Hudson：指美国纽约州境内的哈得逊河。
25. Hotel de Cluny：指巴黎的克吕尼宫，初建于15世纪末叶，现为收藏中世纪艺术品的博物馆。
26. a Caryatid：欧洲古典建筑物中的女像柱，通常为大理石的女性雕像。
27. Nantucketer：南塔克特基特岛上的居民。南塔克特基特岛位于美国马萨诸塞州东南方向，作为避暑胜地而闻名。在小说中，这里是皮阔德号航海的出发点，小说的叙述者在该岛上受聘为船员参加追杀白鲸的航行。

28. the Pequod：皮阔德号，船名，即小说的主人公埃哈伯驾驶出海寻找白鲸的航船。

29. that prudent isle：指南塔克特基特岛，参见注27。

30. a Job's whale：指《圣经》中提及的海中怪兽，参见注8。

31. a seventy-four：意为旧时的战船，因船上通常安装74门火炮。

第五章
亨利·大卫·梭罗 Henry David Thoreau

作者简介

亨利·大卫·梭罗（Henry David Thoreau, 1817—1862），散文家、哲学家、诗人。哈佛大学毕业后曾当过小学教师，但因无法接受约束而在两周后辞职。后在父亲的铅笔厂帮过忙，并与兄弟一起办过3年小学。他与爱默生建立了长期的友谊，成为新英格兰超验主义的重要作家。他对超验主义身体力行，最有代表性的两件事情就是在沃尔登湖畔度过的两年和在监狱度过的一夜。他因为反对美国政府实行奴隶制、对墨西哥发动帝国主义战争而拒绝纳税，因而遭受一夜囚禁，并就此经历写出《论公民的不服从》(On the Duty of Civil Disobedience, 1849）这篇文章，认为人民应该拒绝服从自己认为是不正当的法律。他在文中写道："一个真正自由和开明的国家必须承认个人是一种更高的独立的力量，国家本身的力量和权威来源于个人的力量，个人必须得到与之相应的对待。"他的这篇文章，特别是文中消极反抗或非暴力反抗的观点，极大地影响了托尔斯泰、甘地、马丁·路德·金等社会改革家。梭罗后来逐渐脱离超验主义，成为一位社会活动家。他积极参加废除奴隶制的活动，帮助奴隶沿着"地下铁路"逃往北方，并撰写抨击奴隶制的文章《马萨诸塞州的奴隶制》。他十分崇拜废奴主义者约翰·布朗；在约翰·布朗因武装起义而被美国政府处死之后，他心理上受到重大打击。梭罗一生追求崇高的道德境界，为崇尚物质的美国生活增加了一个精神侧面。

内容提要

选篇摘自《沃尔登》中的第二篇文章"我生活的地方；我为何生活"。为了实践他的超验主义哲学，梭罗曾在马萨诸塞州康科德附近的沃尔登湖畔自建木屋，靠采集野菜、野果，自种豆类而维持生活长达两年之久。他在沃尔登湖畔的生活和思考使他得以完成两部最重要的著作：《在康科德与梅里马克河上一周》（A Week on the Concord and Merrimack River，1849）和《沃尔登》（Walden，1854）。《沃尔登》由18篇文章组成，记录了他所观察到的自然以及他建造木屋、耕种土地、招待朋友等生活情况。书中讴歌了人类与自然的和谐生活，倡导个人主义、自力更生、物质节俭。他试图将身体的物质需要缩小到最低限度，以便在读书、思考、观察自然与自我当中获得最大的精神财富和自由。他也呼吁人们过最简朴的生活，以便节约时间和精力来“过深层次的生活，吮吸出生活的精髓”。他努力发掘美国自然环境在人类教养、心灵塑造等方面的潜能，强调所有人都应该有充分的自由来选择独一无二的生活方式，将自己的生活做成诗、当作艺术。他向人们展示出闲暇、沉思、与大自然和谐共处等的种种益处，为美国自然作家的写作开了先河。在《沃尔登》的数篇文章中，梭罗对工作和闲暇的意义进行了颇有独创性的思考，并描述了自己在尽可能简朴地、自给自足的生活方面所做的试验，强调这项简朴生活的试验绝不是无所事事地与世隔绝。在另一些文章中，梭罗描述了林中生活的细节：他与各种各样的小动物的接触；不同季节中树木与水的不同声音、气味和颜色；大风吹动电报线以及远方的火车汽笛声所奏出的旋律等。梭罗在沃尔登湖畔日复一日的切身经历使该书具有极大的真实感，而文章清晰、直截了当，但又不失文雅的风格，使《沃尔登》达到了文学经典作品的水平。

赏　析

选篇分两个部分：第一部分描述了梭罗对于家园的总体态度和一般寻求，主要刻画了寻找家园的心理过程和精神满足；第二部分则具体描述梭罗在沃尔登湖畔的家园以及这一家园与大自然的融合。

在第一部分，梭罗仔细勘察了许多农场。他用“survey”一词来暗指他本人土地测量员（surveyor）的身份，说自己是所有勘察测量过的土地的君王。梭罗在想象中买下了无数农场，他用商业语言描述了购买农场的过程，但金钱交换实际上并未发生，发生的只是精神财富的增加。他没有买下农场，但保留了景色；就像诗人一样，用韵律这一隐形的篱笆，圈住了农场，得到了田园的精华。在以上描述中，梭罗用日常生活的语言，发掘出了深层的意义。他以“自然诗人”的敏感细腻，改变了通常以人为中心的思维模式，将大自然放到了最重要的地位。他喜欢破旧的房屋、倒塌的栅栏，因为这使他远离以前的房客，而更接近于自然；他喜爱空心的树木，因为这说明他的邻居将是啃啮树木的兔子。他用一个双关词“committed”告诫人们，要过自由、无拘无束“uncommitted”的生活。因为贪婪而受到农场的束缚、而过分投入到农场的事务，就无异于关进牢笼。

在选篇的第二部分，梭罗具体描述了他自己在沃尔登湖畔建立的家园。他所建造的木屋只能遮雨，不能挡风。但在他看来，穿堂而过的风声恰恰是大地音乐的天国乐章，是未被打断的创世纪的诗篇。他与鸟为邻，但并非像一般人一样，将鸟关在笼子里；恰恰相反，他将“关自己的笼子”放在离鸟近的地方。他的这一实践和描述大大影响了现代的自然保护主义者：在现代的野生公园里，野生动物可以四处游荡，而游人则只能在笼子里观赏。梭罗的情感与大自然完全交融，他因此而生活在最吸引他的地方和时代：他的家坐落在宇宙中一个隐秘、常新、未受亵渎的角落。

梭罗的创作表现出对于声音、意象、深层意义、词的细微差别等的高度敏感。他的写作风格乍看起来平铺直叙、直截了当，但实际上，各种巧妙的比喻、词源上的双关语、典故的运用、对传统谚语的灵活运用等，使通常的意义发生了变化或者扭曲，使读者不得不对作品进行重新思考、重新评价。例如在以上选篇中，他 将山峰比喻为天国造币厂所铸造的纯蓝色（true-blue，又有不褪色的蓝色或忠诚的含义）的硬币，将天国、自然与人间联系起来。他将自己比喻为将大地和天空扛在肩上的阿特拉斯，但他所扛起的却是精神的大地和天空。他说诸神之家奥林波斯只不过是无处不在的大地的外表，这既赋予世上万物以灵气，又将诸神融入了自然与人间。

Walden

Chapter 2 (Excerpt)

WHERE I LIVED, AND WHAT I LIVED FOR

At a certain season of our life we are accustomed to consider[1] every spot a possible site of a house. I have thus surveyed the country on every side within a dozen miles of where I live. In imagination I have bought all the farms in succession[2], for all were to be bought[3], and I knew their price. I walked over farmer's premises[4], tasted his wild apples, discoursed on husbandry with him, took his farm at his price, at any price[5], mortgaging it to him in my mind; even put a higher price on it,—took everything but a deed of it[6]—took his word for his deed[7], for I dearly love to talk,—cultivated it, and him[8] too to some extent, I trust, and withdrew when I had enjoyed it long enough, leaving him to carry it on. This experience entitled me to be regarded as a sort of real-estate broker by my friends. Wherever I sat, there I might live, and the landscape radiated from me accordingly[9]. What is a house but a sedes[10], a seat?—better if a country seat. I discovered many a site for a house not likely to be soon improved, which some might have thought too far from the village, but to my eyes the village was too far from it. Well, there I might live, I said; and there I did live, for an hour, a summer and a winter life; saw how I could let the years run off, buffet the winter through[11], and see the spring come in. The future inhabitants of this region, wherever they may place their houses, may be sure that they have been anticipated[12]. An afternoon sufficed to lay out the land into orchard, wood-lot, and pasture, and to decide what fine oaks or pines should be left to stand before the door, and whence each blasted tree could be seen to the best advantage[13]; and then I let it lie, fallow perchance, for a man is rich in proportion to the number of things which he can afford to let alone.

My imagination carried me so far that I even had the refusal of several farms, —the refusal was all I wanted, —but I never got my fingers burned by actual possession. The nearest that I came to actual possession was when I bought the Hollowell Place[14], and had begun to sort my seeds, and collected materials with which to make a wheelbarrow to carry it on or off with[15]; but before the owner gave me a deed of it, his wife—every man has such a wife—changed her mind and wished to keep it, and he offered me ten dollars to release him. Now, to speak the truth, I had but ten cents in the world, and it surpassed my arithmetic to tell, if I was that man who had ten cents, or who had a. farm, or ten dollars, or all together.[16] However, I let him keep the ten dollars and the farm too, for I had carried it far enough; or rather, to be generous, I sold him the farm for just what I gave for it, and, as he was not a rich man, made him a present of ten dollars, and still had my ten cents, and seeds, and materials for a wheelbarrow left. I found thus that I had been a rich man without any damage to my poverty. But I retained the landscape, and I have since annually carried off what it yielded without a wheelbarrow. With respect to landscapes,—

"I am monarch of all I survey, My right there is none to dispute." [17]

I have frequently seen a poet withdraw, having enjoyed the most valuable part of a farm, while the crusty farmer supposed that he had got a few wild apples only. Why, the owner does not know it for many years when a poet has put his farm in rhyme, the most admirable kind of invisible fence, has fairly impounded it, milked it, skimmed it, and got all the cream, and left the farmer only the skimmed milk.

The real attractions of the Hollowell farm, to me, were: its complete retirement, being about two miles from the village, half a mile from the nearest neighbor, and separated from the highway by a broad field; its bounding on the river, which the owner said protected it by its fogs from frosts in the spring, though that was nothing to me; the gray color and ruinous state of the house and barn, and the dilapidated fences, which put such an interval between me and the last occupant; the hollow and lichen-covered apple trees, gnawed by rabbits, showing what kind of neighbors I should have; but above all, the recollection I had of it from my earliest voyages up the river, when the house was concealed behind a dense grove of red maples, through which I heard the house-dog bark. I was in haste to buy it, before the proprietor finished getting out some rocks, cutting down the hollow apple trees, and grubbing up some young birches which had sprung up in the pasture, or, in short, had made any more of his improvements. To enjoy these advantages I was ready to carry it on; like Atlas[18], to take the world on my shoulders,—I never heard what compensation he received for that,—and do all those things which had no other motive or excuse but that I might pay for it and be unmolested in my possession of it; for I knew all the while that it would yield the most abundant crop of the kind I wanted, if I could only afford to let it alone. But it turned out as I have said.

All that I could say, then, with respect to farming on a large scale—I have always cultivated a garden—was, that I had had my seeds ready. Many think that seeds improve with age. I have no doubt that time discriminates between the good and the bad; and when at last I shall plant, I shall be less likely to be disappointed. But I would say to my fellows, once for all, as long as possible live free and uncommitted. It makes but little difference whether you are committed to a farm or the county jail.

Old Cato, whose "De Re Rustica" [19] is my "Cultivator," says,—and the only translation I have seen makes sheer nonsense of the passage,—"When you think of getting a farm turn it thus in your mind, not to buy greedily; nor spare your pains to look at it, and do not think it enough to go round it once. The oftener you go there the more it will please you, if it is good." I think I shall not buy greedily, but go round and round it as long as I live, and be buried in it first, that it may please me the more at last.

The present was my next experiment of this kind, which I purpose to describe more at length, for convenience putting the experience of two years into one[20]. As

I have said, I do not propose to write an ode to dejection, but to brag as lustily as chanticleer in the morning, standing on his roost, if only to wake my neighbors up.

When first I took up my abode in the woods, that is, began to spend my nights as well as days there, which, by accident, was on Independence Day, or the Fourth of July, 1845, my house was not finished for winter, but was merely a defence against the rain, without plastering or chimney, the walls being of rough, weather-stained boards, with wide chinks, which made it cool at night. The upright white hewn studs and freshly planed door and window casings gave it a clean and airy look, especially in the morning, when its timbers were saturated with dew, so that I fancied that by noon some sweet gum would exude from them. To my imagination it retained throughout the day more or less of this auroral character, reminding me of a certain house on a mountain which I had visited a year before. This was an airy and unplastered cabin, fit to entertain a travelling god, and where a goddess might trail her garments. The winds which passed over my dwelling were such as sweep over the ridges of mountains, bearing the broken strains, or celestial parts only, of terrestrial music. The morning wind forever blows, the poem of creation is uninterrupted; but few are the ears that hear it. Olympus[21] is but the outside of the earth everywhere.

The only house I had been the owner of before, if I except a boat, was a tent, which I used occasionally when making excursions in the summer, and this is still rolled up in my garret; but the boat, after passing from hand to hand, has gone down the stream of time. With this more substantial shelter about me, I had made some progress toward settling in the world. This frame, so slightly clad, was a sort of crystallization around me, and reacted on the builder. It was suggestive somewhat as a picture in outlines. I did not need to go outdoors to take the air, for the atmosphere within had lost none of its freshness. It was not so much within-doors as behind a door where I sat, even in the rainiest weather. The Harivansa[22] says, "An abode without birds is like a meat without seasoning." Such was not my abode, for I found myself suddenly neighbor to the birds; not by having imprisoned one, but having caged myself near them. I was not only nearer to some of those which commonly frequent the garden and the orchard, but to those wilder and more thrilling songsters of the forest which never, or rarely, serenade a villager,—the wood thrush, the veery, the scarlet tanager, the field sparrow, the whip-poor-will, and many others.

I was seated by the shore of a small pond, about a mile and a half south of the village of Concord and somewhat higher than it, in the midst of an extensive wood between that town and Lincoln, and about two miles south of that our only field known to fame, Concord Battle Ground[23]; but I was so low in the woods that the opposite shore, half a mile off, like the rest, covered with wood, was my most distant horizon. For the first week, whenever I looked out on the pond it impressed me like a tarn high up on the side of a mountain, its bottom far above the surface of other lakes, and, as the sun arose, I saw it throwing off its nightly clothing of mist, and here and there, by degrees, its soft ripples or its smooth reflecting surface was revealed, while the mists, like ghosts, were stealthily withdrawing in every direction into the woods, as at the breaking up of some nocturnal conventicle. The very dew seemed to hang upon the trees later into the day than usual, as on the sides of mountains.

This small lake was of most value as a neighbor in the intervals of a gentle rain-storm in August, when, both air and water being perfectly still, but the sky overcast, mid-afternoon had all the serenity of evening, and the wood thrush sang around, and was heard from shore to shore. A lake like this is never smoother than at such a time; and the clear portion of the air above it being shallow and darkened by clouds, the water, full of light and reflections, becomes a lower heaven itself, so much the more important. From a hill-top nearby, where the wood had been recently cut off, there was a pleasing vista southward across the pond, through a wide indentation in the hills which form the shore there, where their opposite sides sloping toward each other suggested a stream flowing out in that direction through a wooded valley, but stream there was none. That way I looked between and over the near green hills to some distant and higher ones in the horizon, tinged with blue. Indeed, by standing on tiptoe I could catch a glimpse of some of the peaks of the still bluer and more distant mountain ranges in the northwest, those true-blue coins from heaven's own mint, and also of some portion of the village. But in other directions, even from this point, I could not see over or beyond the woods which surrounded me. It is well to have some water in your neighborhood, to give buoyancy to and float the earth. One value even of the smallest well is, that when you look into it you see that earth is not continent but insular. This is as important as that it keeps butter cool. When I looked across the pond from this peak toward the Sudbury meadows, which in time of flood I distinguished elevated perhaps by a mirage in their seething valley, like a coin in a basin, all the earth beyond the pond appeared like a thin crust insulated and floated even by this small sheet of intervening water, and I was reminded that this on which I dwelt was but dry land.

Though the view from my door was still more contracted, I did not feel crowded or confined in the least. There was pasture enough for my imagination. The low shrub oak plateau to which the opposite shore arose stretched away toward the prairies of the West and the steppes of Tartary, affording ample room for all the roving families of men. "There are none happy in the world but beings who enjoy freely a vast horizon,"—said Damodara[24], when his herds required new and larger pastures.

Both place and time were changed, and I dwelt nearer to those parts of the universe and to those eras in history which had most attracted me. Where I lived was as far off as many a region viewed.nightly by astronomers. We are wont to imagine rare and delectable places in some remote and more celestial corner of the system, behind the constellation of Cassiopeia's Chair[25], far from noise and disturbance. I discovered that my house actually had its site in such a withdrawn, but forever new and unprofaned, part of the universe. If it were worth the while to settle in those parts near to the Pleiades or the Hyades, to Aldebaran or Altair[26] then I was really there, or at an equal remoteness from the life which I had left behind, dwindled and twinkling with as fine a ray to my nearest neighbor, and to be seen only in moonless nights by him. Such was that part of creation where I had squatted;—

Question:

"There was a shepherd that did live,
And held his thoughts as high
As were the mounts whereon his flocks
Did hourly feed him by."

What should we think of the shepherd's life if his flocks always wandered to higher pastures than his thoughts?

Questions:

1. Where indeed did Thoreau live, both at a physical level and at a spiritual level?
2. Had Thoreau ever bought a farm? Why did he enjoy the act of buying?
3. Is it significant that Thoreau mentioned the Fourth of July as the day on which he began to stay in the woods? Why?
4. How could you answer the question Thoreau asked at the end of this selection?

注　释

1. to be accustomed to: 在现代英语中，该词组后一般应跟着动名词，意思是"习惯于做某事"，例如："accustomed to making decisions"（习惯于做决定）。但在较早的英语中，也能见到后面跟不定式的情况，例如："accustomed to paint their faces before battle"（作战之前有涂抹面部的习俗）。

2. in succession: 按顺序。全句的意思是：“在想象中，我已经依次买下了所有的农场。”
3. be to: 可以表示意图、可能性、推测、责任、安排等，在此表示意图。
4. premises: 房屋及其附属的土地。在现代英语中，该词用于这一意义时必须用复数。
5. ... took his farm at his price, at any price...: 按他所开的价，不管他开什么价，买下他的农场。
6. ... took everything but a deed of it...: 买下了所有东西，只是没有立契约。
7. ... took his word for his deed...: 把他的话当成他的契约。
8. cultivated it, and him: 耕耘了这片田地，也耕耘了他的心田。
9. Wherever I sat, there I might live, and the landscape radiated from me accordingly.: 我坐在哪儿，就可以住在哪儿，哪儿的风景就会相应地以我为中心向四周散发光芒。
10. sedes:座位。
11. ... buffet the winter through...: 搏斗着度过冬天。
12. ... they have been anticipated...: 在他们之前就有人住过那个地方了。
13. ... whence each blasted tree could be seen to the best advantage: 从哪个地方才能最好地看到每一棵饱经风霜的枯树。
14. Hollowell Place: 康科德附近的一个老农场。
15. ... to make a wheelbarrow to carry it on or off with...: 既有字面上的具体意思，又有抽象的含义：1）做一辆小推车来把它推来推去；2）做一辆小推车来实施或者完成这项计划。
16. ... it surpassed my arithmetic to tell, if I was that man who had ten cents, or who had a farm, or ten dollars, or all together.: 我那点算术算不清楚我到底是一个有一角钱，还是一个有整个田园，还是一个有十元钱，还是拥有这一切的人。
17. “I am monarch of all I survey. / My right there is none to dispute.” : 引自威廉·柯珀(1731—1800),“据说是亚历山大·塞尔扣克所作的诗”。梭罗将

"survey" 一词写成斜体，以作为双关语暗指他本人测量员（surveyor）的职业。

18. Atlas（阿特拉斯）：希腊神话中的神，他将大地和天空扛在肩上。
19. Old Cato: 大加图（Marcus Porcius Cato, 234 B.C.—149 B.C.），罗马政治家、演说家、拉丁散文作家。De Re Rustica, 又称De Agricultura（《农书》，成书约公元前160年）是他流传至今的唯一著作。
20. putting the experience of two years into one: 为了使《沃尔登》前后统一，梭罗将他两年零两个月的生活经历浓缩为一年。
21. Olympus: 奥林波斯，希腊神话中诸神之家。
22. Harivansa: 哈利梵萨，印度5世纪的宗教史诗。
23. Concord Battle Ground: 美国独立战争时期的著名战场（1775年4月19日）。
24. Damodara: 达摩达拉，《哈利梵萨》中的神。
25. Cassiopeia's Chair: 仙后座。
26. the Pleiades, the Hyades, Aldebaran, Altair: 昴星团，毕星团，毕宿五，牵牛星，皆为星座或星球之名。

第六章
马克·吐温Mark Twain

作者简介

马克·吐温（Mark Twain,1835—1910）是萨缪尔·朗荷恩·克莱门斯（Samuel Langhorne Clemens）的笔名，小说家。萨缪尔少年时居住在密苏里州密西西比河畔的小镇汉尼拔，11岁丧父，13岁到印刷所当学徒，长大后离开家乡，曾在密西西比河上做汽轮舵手，也曾参加采矿投机。

1865年他的第一部幽默短篇《加拉维拉县驰名的跳蛙》（*The Celebrated Jumping Frog of Calaveras County*）问世。1869年，游记《傻瓜出国记》（*The Innocents Abroad*）发表，奠定了他的幽默大师地位。1873年，他与查尔斯·华纳合作发表了他的第一部长篇《镀金时代》（*The Gilded Age*）。这部小说尖刻讥讽了南北战争后社会道德现状。虽然小说故事结构等方面均差强人意，但仍不失为美国现实主义文学开山之作。1876年发表充满童趣和田园诗意的《汤姆·索亚历险记》（The Adventures of Tom Sawyer）。以后8年中，吐温发表了《密西西比河上》（*Life on the Mississippi*,1883）并完成了长篇小说《哈克贝利·费恩历险记》（*The Adventures of Huckleberry Finn*,1884）。故事讲述男孩哈克·贝里和黑奴吉姆乘木筏沿密西西比河而下的前后经历。其后马克·吐温的主要著作包括《亚瑟王朝廷上的康尼狄格州美国佬》（*A Connecticut Yankee in King Arthur's Court*,1889），《傻瓜威尔逊》（*The Tragedy of Pudd'nhead Wilson*,1894）和《败坏了哈德莱堡的人》（*The Man That Corrupted Hadleyburg*,1900）。

马克·吐温对美国文学的贡献举足轻重。他以前的主要美国作家受欧洲文学影响较大，而他的思维方式、价值观、创作语言、甚至他的幽默都是地道美国土产。“乡土特色”(local color)是他的小说的突出特点，表现了一个地区的语言特点、习俗和生活方式。同时，他的口语体散文形式成为美国口语体文学传统的发端，安德森、海明威、艾略特、福克纳、塞林格等都在不同程度上受到他的影响。福克纳曾说：“我认识马克·吐温是第一个名副其实的美国作家，我们都是他的传人。”

赏 析

《加拉维拉县驰名的跳蛙》取材于淘金者流传的夸张故事。故事的第一人称叙事者(first-person narrator)“我”显然是个知识阶层的绅士，这一点不难从其遣词造句中看出。而讲跳蛙故事的人确是一个采矿区粗人维勒。“我”受朋友之托去找维勒，向他打听一个姓斯迈里的人。而维勒却给他讲起另一个姓斯迈里的人和他的许多故事，“我”完全搞不懂维勒为什么要讲这些与他毫不相关而又无聊之至的故事，最后一逃了之。

从《跳蛙》故事叙述上看，这一方法创造出故事叙述框架和讲故事者与故事内容之间的不协调，甚至荒谬。这就产生了马克·吐温在《怎样讲故事》中谈到的所谓美国式幽默效果，其最基本的原则是讲故事者一定要显得自己并不意识到故事可笑，必须完全不动声色，从而产生讲故事过程本身和故事内容之间的不协调，已达到幽默效果。当然，维勒的故事叙述框架不仅仅是不动声色，而是从多个层面制造不协调：讲者听者各行其是，而叙述框架与幽默故事本身不协调的效果由于跳蛙故事的内容特点得到进一步强化。维勒的故事自始至终表达了对人性和其他生灵的热情关注，常常短短数语，人情物欲，动物灵性跃然纸上，从而使人性与自然的谐趣天成与讲者听者浑然不觉其幽默情调恰为对照。

在故事结构和内容上，读者可注意到两个层面上的计谋：“我”大概中了“我”的朋友的圈套，赌客们中了斯迈里的圈套，小动物中了人的圈套，而斯迈里又中了“陌生人”的圈套，从而形成了圈套套圈套，欺骗套欺骗的效果，“陌生人”胜了常胜赌家，而粗人是否又胜书生一筹呢?

如果从另一个层面上理解，体力劳动阶层的话题和交流方式使知识阶层困惑不解甚至不屑一顾，但其中道理和意义却不言自明，而且往往更符合人情常理。不同社会阶层之间的话语障碍同时也构成故事的不协调因素，从而获得幽默讽刺效果。在美国文学传统中，以马克·吐温、海明威等为代表的作家表现出美国价值传统中的实用主义倾向，具体表现为对实际体力参与和实际创造物质财富的崇尚，以及对不切实际的知识和理智的讥讽和鄙视。在当时典型美国人的观念中，人生的真正目的就是挣钱，而且最体面的挣钱方式是商业冒险。这一点在马克·吐温身上表现得十分明显。他又清楚地看到这一价值观念的可笑荒唐之处。而《跳蛙》中斯迈里的投机心态正是时代的幽默注脚。

The Celebrated Jumping Frog of Calaveras County

In compliance with the request of a friend of mine, who wrote me from the East, I called on good-natured, garrulous old Simon Wheeler, and inquired after my friend's friend, Leonidas W. Smiley, as requested to do, and I hereunto append the result. I have a lurking suspicion that Leonidas W. Smiley is a myth; that my friend never knew such a personage; and that he only conjectured that, if I asked old Wheeler about him, it would remind him of his infamous Jim Smiley, and he would go to work and bore me to death with some exasperating reminiscence of him as long and tedious as it should be useless to me. If that was the design, it succeeded.

I found Simon Wheeler dozing comfortably by the bar-room stove of the dilapidated tavern in the decayed mining camp of Angel's, and I noticed that he was fat and bald-headed, and had an expression of winning gentleness and simplicity upon his tranquil countenance. He roused up and gave me good day. I told him a friend of mine had commissioned me to make some inquiries about a cherished companion of his boyhood named Leonidas W. Smiley—Rev. Leonidas W. Smiley, a young minister of the Gospel, who he had heard was at one time a resident of Angel's Camp. I added that if Mr. Wheeler could tell me anything about this Rev. Leonidas W. Smiley, I would feel under many obligations to him.

Simon Wheeler backed me into a corner and blockaded me there with his chair, and then sat down and reeled off the monotonous narrative which follows this paragraph. He never smiled, he never frowned, he never changed his voice from the gentle-flowing key to which he tuned the initial sentence, he never betrayed the slightest suspicion of enthusiasm; but all through the interminable narrative there ran a vein of impressive earnestness and sincerity, which showed me plainly that, so far from his imagining that there was anything ridiculous or funny about his story, he regarded it as a really important matter, and admired its two heroes as men of transcendent genius in finesse. I let him go on in his own way, and never interrupted him once.

"Rev. Leonidas W. H'm , Reverend Le—Well, There was a feller here once by the name of Jim Smiley, in the winter of '49—or may be it was the spring of '50—I don't recollect exactly, somehow, though what makes me think it was one or the other is because I remember the big flume warn't finished when he first came to the camp; but anyway, he was the curiousest man about always betting on anything that turned up you ever see, if he could get anybody to bet on the other side; and if he couldn't he'd change sides. Any way that suited the other man would suit him—any way just so's he got a bet, he was satisfied. But still he was lucky, uncommon lucky; he most always come out winner. He was always ready and laying for a chance; there couldn't be no solit'ry thing mentioned but that feller'd offer to bet on it, and take ary side you please, as I was just telling you. If there was a horse-race, you'd find him flush or you'd find him busted at the end of it; if there was a dog-fight, he'd bet on it; if there was a chicken-fight, he'd bet on it; if there was a chicken-fight, he'd bet on it; why, if there was two birds setting on a fence, he would bet you which one would fly first; or if there was a camp-meeting, he would be there reg'lar to bet on Parson Walker, which he judged to be the best exhorter about here, and so he was too, and a good man. If he even seen a straddle-bug start to go anywheres, he would bet you how long it would take him to get to—to wherever he was going to, and if you took him up, he would foller that straddle-bug to Mexico but what he would find out where he was bound for and how long he was on the road[21]. Lots of the boys here has seen[22] that Smiley and can tell you about him. Why, it never made no difference[23] to him—he'd bet on any thing—the dangest feller[24]. Parson Walker's wife laid very sick[25] once, for a good while, and it seemed as if they warn's going to save her[26]; but one morning he come in[27], and Smiley up and asked[28] how she was, and he said she was consid'rable better[29]—thank the Lord for his inf'nit'mercy30—and coming on so smart31 that with the blessing of Prov'dence[32] she'd get well yet; and Smiley, before he thought, says[33], "Well, I'll risk two- and-a-half she don't, any way."

"Thish-yer Smiley[35] had a mare—the boys called her the fifteen- minute nag, but that was only in fun, you know, because of course, she was faster than that—and he used to win money on that horse, for all she was so slow and always had the asthma, or the distemper, or the consumption, or something of that kind. They used to give her two or three hundred yards' start[36], and then pass her under way; but always at the fag-end of the race she'd get excited and desperate like, and come cavorting and straddling up, and scattering her legs around limber, sometimes in the air, and sometimes out to one side amongst the fences, and kicking up m-o-r-e dust and raising m-o-r-e racket with her coughing and sneezing and blowing her nose—and always fetch up[37] at the stand just about a neck ahead, as near as you could cipher it down[38]."

"And he had a little small bull-pup, that to look at him you'd think he warn's worth a cent but to set around and look ornery and lay for a chance to steal something. But as soon as money was up on him[39] he was a different dog; his under-jaw'd begin to stick out like the fo'castle[40] of a steamboat, and his teeth would uncover and shine like the furnaces. And a dog might tackle him and bully-rag him, and bite him, and throw him over his shoulder two or three times, and Andrew Jackson[41]—which was the name of the pup—Andrew Jackson would never let on but what he was satisfied, and hadn't expected nothing else—and the bets being doubled and doubled on the other side all the time, till the money was all up[43]; and then all of a sudden he would grab that other dog jest[44] by the j'int[45] of his hind leg and freeze on it—not chew, you understand, but only jest grip and hang on till they thronged up the sponge[46], if it was a year[47]. Smiley always come out[48] winner on that pup, till he harnessed a dog once that didn't have no hind legs[49], because they'd been sawed off in a circular saw, and when the thing had gone along far enough, and the money was all up, and he come to make a snatch for his pet holt[50], he see[51] in a minute how he'd been imposed on[52], and how the other dog had him in the door[53], so to speak, and he 'peared[54] surprised, and then he looked sorter[55] discouraged-like, and didn't try no more[56] to win the fight, and so he got shucked out bad. He gave Smiley a look, as much as to say his heart was broke[57], and it was his fault, for putting up a dog that hadn't no hind legs for him to take bolt of, which was his main dependence in a fight, and then he limped off a piece[58] and laid down[59] and died. It was a good pup, was that Andrew Jackson, and would have made a name for hisself[60] if he'd lived, for the stuff was in him and he had genius—I know it, because he hadn't had no opportunitics[61] to speak of, and it don't stand to reason[62] that a dog could make such a fight as he could under them circumstances[63] if he hadn't no talent[64]. It always makes me feel sorry when I think of that last fight of his'n[65], and the way it turned out."

"Well, thish-yer Smiley had rat-tarriers, and chicken cocks, and tomcats, and all of them kind of things[66], till you couldn't rest, and you couldn't fetch nothing for him to bet on but he'd match you[67]. He ketched[68] a frog one day, and took him home, and said he cal'lated[69] to educate him; and so he never done nothing[70] for three months but set in his back yard and learn that frog to jump[71]. And you bet you[72] he did learn him[73], too. He'd give him a little punch behind, and the next minute you'd see that frog whirling in the air like a doughnut—see him turn one summerset, or may be a couple, if he got a good start[74], and come down flat-footed and all right[75], like a cat. He got him up so in the matter of ketching flies[76], and kep'[77] him in practice so constant, that he'd nail a fly every time as far as[78] he could see him. Smiley said all a frog wanted was education, and he could do' most[79] anything—and I believe him. Why, I've seen him set Dan'l Webster[80] down here on this floor—Dan'l Webster was the name of the frog—and sing out, 'Flies, Dan'l, flies!' and quicker'n[81] you could wink, he'd spring straight up and snake a fly off'n[82] the counter there, and flop down on the floor ag'in[83] as solid as a gob of mud, and fall to scratching the side of his head with his hind foot as indifferent[84] as if he hadn't no idea[85] he'd been doin'[86] any more'n[87] any frog might do. You never see a frog so modest and straightfor'ard[88] as he was, for all he was so gifted. And when it come[89] to fair and square jumping on a dead level[90], he could get over more ground at one straddle than any animal of his breed you ever see. Jumping on a dead level was his strong suit, you understand; and when it come to that[91], Smiley would ante up money on him as long as he had a red[92]. Smiley was monstrous proud of his frog, and well he might be, for fellers[93] that had traveled and been everywheres[94], all said he laid over any frog that ever they see."

"Well, Smiley kep' the beast in a little lattice box, and he used to fetch him downtown sometimes and lay for a bet. One day a feller—a stranger in the camp, he was—come acrost him with his box, and says:" What might it be that you've got in the box?"

"And Smiley says, sorter indifferent- like, "It might be a parrot, or it might be a canary, may be, but it ain't -it's only just a frog."

"And the feller took it, and looked at it careful, and turned it round this way and that, and says, "H'm—so 'tis. Well, what's he good for?"

"Well,Smiley says, easy and careless, "He's good enough for one thing, I should judge—he can outjump any frog in Calaveras county."

"The feller took the box again, and took another long, particular look, and give it back to Smiley, and says, very deliberate, "Well, he says,I don't see no p'ints about that frog that's any better'n any other frog."

"Maybe you don't," Smiley says. "Maybe you understand frogs, and maybe you don't understand 'em; may be you've had experience, and maybe you an't only a amature, as it were. Anyways, I've got my opinion, and I'll risk forty dollars that he can out-jump any frog in Calaveras county."

And the feller studied a minute, and then says, kinder sadlike, "Well, I'm only a stranger here, and I an't got no frog; but if I had a frog, I'd bet you."

And then Smiley says, "That's all right—that's all right—if you'll hold my box a minute, I'll go and get you a frog." And so the feller took the box, and put up his forty dollars along with Smiley's, and set down to wait.

So he set there a good while thinking and thinking to hisself, and then he got the frog out and prized his mouth open and took a teaspoon and filled him full of quail shot—filled him pretty near up to his chin—and set him on the floor. Smiley he went to the swamp and slopped around in the mud for a long time, and finally he ketched a frog, and fetched him in, and give him to this feller, and says:

"Now, if you're ready, set him alongside of Dan'l, with his fore- paws just even with Dan'l's, and I'll give the word." Then he says, "One—two –three—git!" and him and the feller touched up the frogs from behind, and the new frog hopped off lively, but Dan'l give a heave, and hysted up his shoulders—so—like a Frenchman, but it warn's no use—he couldn't budge; he was planted as solid as a church ,and he couldn't no more stir than115 if he was anchored out. Smiley was a good deal surprised, and he was disgusted too, but he didn't have no idea116 what the matter was, of course.

The feller took the money and started away; and when he was going out at the door, he sorter jerked his thumb over his shoulder—so—at Dan'l, and says again, very deliberate, "Well, he say`s, I don't see no p'ints about that frog that's any better'n any other frog."

Smiley he stood scratching his head and looking down at Dan'l a long time, and at last he says, "I do wonder what in the nation that frog throw'd off117 for —I wonder if there ain't something the matter with him—he 'pears 119to look mighty baggy, somehow." And he ketched Dan'l by the nap120 of the neck, and hefted him , and says, "Why, blame my cats, if he don't weigh five pounds!121" and turned him upside down and he belched out a double handful of shot. And then he see122 how it was, and he was the maddest man—he set the frog down and took out after 123that feller, but he never ketched him. And-

Here Simon Wheeler heard his name called from the front yard, and got up to see what was wanted.]And turning to me as he moved away, he said: "Just set where you are, stranger, and rest easy—I an't going to be gone a second."

But, by your leave, I did not think that a continuation of the history of the enterprising vagabond Jim Smiley would be likely to afford me much information concerning the Rev. Leonidas W. Smiley, and so I started away.

At the door I met the sociable Wheeler returning, and he buttonholed me and recommenced:

"Well, thish-yer .Smiley had a yeller124 one-eyed cow that didn't have no tail, only jest125 a short stump like a bannanner, and—"

"Oh! hang Smiley and his afflicted cow!" I muttered, good-naturedly, and bidding the old gentleman good day, I departed.

Question:

1. Why do you think Mr.Wheeler is so eager to tell these stories?
2. Does his audience share his enthusiasm in telling the stories?
3. Do you think the narrator and his listener ever suspect the presence of humor? Why? How do you interpret their interactions?

注　释

1. ...I hereunto append the result.：I append the result to this writing; hereunto：hereto（法律文书常用语，意思是：to this document）。
2. go to work：开始（作某事）。
3. If that was the design，it succeeded.：如果这是其本意，他达到了目的。
4. Winning：讨人喜欢的。
5. Feller：fellow
6. Warn't：wasn't
7. When he first come：when he first came
8. So's：so long as
9. Uncommon lucky：uncommonly lucky
10. most always：almost always
11. there couldn't be no solit'ry thing mentioned but that feller'd offer to bet on it：there could be no solitary thing mentioned which that fellow would noot offer to bet on; but：that not; solitary：single
12. ary：any
13. flush：喜形于色。
14. busted：输的精光。
15. if there was two birds setting on a fence：if there were two birds sitting on a fence
16. camp-meeting：野营布道会。
17. reg'lar：regularly
18. straddie bug：屎壳郎。
19. anywheres：anywhere
20. if you took him up：如果你同意跟他打赌。
21. ...he would foller... on the road.：他就是跟着那只屎壳郎一直到墨西哥，也

一定要弄清它去什么地方，路上要走多久。Foller：follow；but what：but that

22. Lots of the boys here has seen：Lots of the boys here have seen
23. ...it never made no difference...：...it never made any difference
24. the dangest feller：the most damned fellow; dang：damned
25. laid very sick：lay very sick
26. ...it seemed as if they warn't going to save her...：看样子她没救了；they warn't：they weren't
27. ...he come in：...he came in
28. Smiley up and asked：Smiley came up and asked
29. ...she was consid'rable better...：...she was considerably better.
30. Inf'nit' mercy：infinite mercy
31. coming on so smart：she was coming on so smart（她的情形很不错）。
32. Prov'dence：Providence
33. Smiley,...,says：Smily,...,said
34. she don't：she doesn't
35. Thish-yer Smiley：This here Smiley；This Smiley
36. give her two or three hundred yards' start：刚好让你能看清楚。
37. fetch up：到达。
38. as near as you could cipher it down：刚好让你能看清楚。
39. money was up on him：赌注压在它身上。
40. fo'castle：forecastle
41. Andrew Jackson：安德鲁 · 杰克逊（1767—1845），第七任美国总统，民主党人，当选总统后加强联邦政府权力，因此他的反对者称他为"安德鲁王"（King Andrew）.
42. would never let on but what he was satisfied, and hadn't expected nothing else
43. till the money was all up：直到钱全都押上了。
44. jest：just

45. j'int：joint

46. throwed up the sponge：throw in the towel; 认输(拳击比赛中，一方扔出海绵或毛巾表示认输); throwed up：threw up

47. if it was a year：even if it was a year

48. come out winner：came out winner

49. till he harnessed a dog once that didn't have no hind legs：till he was once pitted against a dog that had no hind legs

50. pet holt：pet hold ;爱咬之处

51. he see：he saw

52. he'd been imposed on：它受骗了。

53. had him in the door：把它难住了

54. 'peared：appeared

55. sorter：sort of

56. didn't try no more：didn't try any more

57. his heart was broke：his heart was broken

58. limped off a piece：一瘸一拐走到一边。

59. laid down：lay down

60. hisself：himself

61. hadn't no opportunities：had no opportunities

62. it don't stand to reason：it doesn't stand to reason

63. them circumstances：these circumstances

64. hadn't no talent：had no talent

65. his'n：his

66. all of them kind of things：all of these kind of things

67. you couldn't fetch nothing for him to bet on but he'd match you：you could fetch nothing for him to bet on but he would match you;不管你拿什么和他打赌，他总能赢你。

68. ketched：caught

69. cal'lated：calculated

70. never done nothing：did nothng

71. learn that frog to jump：taught that frog to jump

72. you bet you：you bet

73. learn him：teach him

74. if he got a good start：如果跳好了

75. come down flat-footed and all right：落下来四脚着地，稳稳当当。

76. He got him up so in the matter of ketching flies：他教会它抓苍蝇；ketching：catching

77. kep'：kept

78. as fur as：as far as

79. 'most：almost

80. Dan'l Webster：Daniel Webster（1782—1852）.美国政治家，演说家，辉格党（美国共和党前身）领袖，主张保护州权，主张各州有权不执行国会法令。马克·吐温家人支持该政党。

81. quicker'n：quicker than

82. off'n：off on

83. ag'in：again

84. as indifferent：as indifferently

85. hadn't no idea

86. doin'：doing

87. more'n：more than

88. straightfor'ard：straightforward

89. it come：it came

90. jumping on a dead level：并肩起跳

91. it come to that：it came to that

92. a red：a cent

93. fellers：fellows

94. everywheres：everywhere
95. kep'：kept
96. come acrost：came/comes across
97. it ain't：it isn't
98. looked at it careful：looked at it carefully
99. so 'tis：so it is
100. give it back：gave it back
101. says, very deliberate：said, very deliberately
102. I don't see no p'ints：I don't see any points
103. that's any better'n any other frog：that are any better than any other frog
104. 'em：them
105. ain't：are
106. a amature：an amateur
107. Anyways：Anyway
108. kinder sadlike：kind of sadlike
109. ain't：haven't
110. set down：sat down
111. git：get;go
112. him and the feller touched：he and the fellow touched
113. hysted：hoisted
114. it warn't no use：it was no use
115. couldn't no more stir than：couldn't stir any more than
116. didn't have no idea
117. throw'd off：threw off
118. there ain't：there isn't
119. 'pears：appears
120. nap：nape
121. "Why blame my cats if he don't weigh five pounds!"：它要没有五磅重才

怪呢!

122. took out after：开始去追。

123. yaller：yellow

124. jest：见注释44

125. bannanner：banana

There are several kinds of stories, but only one difficult—the humorous.

A classic is something that everybody wants to have read and nobody wants to read

—Mark Twain

第七章
弗·斯科特·菲茨杰拉德F. Scott Fitzgerald

作者简介

弗·斯科特·菲茨杰拉德（F. Scott Fitzgerald, 1896—1940）出身于一个破落的士绅家庭，在母亲娘家的资助下上了普林斯顿大学。1917年，美国宣布对德作战，他辍学参军，在南方受训时爱上富家女泽尔达，但后者因他没有发达的事业而与他解除婚约。1920年3月，他出版了第一部小说《人间天堂》（This Side of Paradise，1920），一鸣惊人，名利双收，并与泽尔达结婚。婚后他和泽尔达的生活奢华无度，成为美国战后寻求刺激和享乐思潮的代表人物。他在20年代初发表的第二部小说《漂亮的冤家》（The Beautiful and Damned, 1922）和短篇小说集《姑娘们与哲学家们》（Flappers and Philosophers, 1920）与《爵士乐时代的故事》（Tales of the Jazz Age, 1922）真实地反映了爵士时代的风貌。1924年他们去巴黎，结识了斯泰因、庞德、海明威等一批"迷惘的一代"的旅欧美国作家，并创作了《了不起的盖茨比》（*The Great Gatzby*, 1925）。这部小说入木三分地刻画了美国一战后的所谓"喧嚣的20年代"和"爵士乐时代"追求金钱和享乐的潮流，以冷静批判的笔触反思社会现实和浮华表面下蕴藏的精神危机和"美国梦"理想的破灭。几年后，泽尔达因精神病住院治疗，菲茨杰拉德的经济状况日见窘迫。1934年，他的另一部重要小说《夜色温柔》（*Tender Is the Night*, 1934）出版，但并没有获得预期的成功。为了维持生计，他只得为好莱坞写电影脚本。在这时期他反思自己一生，写了不少散文。1940年，他死于心脏病。他的好友，大批评家爱德蒙·威尔逊把他的散文结集出版，题名为《崩溃》（The Crack-Up, 1945）。

内容提要

选篇为菲茨杰拉德的代表作《了不起的盖茨比》的最后一章第九章。

小说主人公盖茨比出身贫寒，但从小心高志远，坚信靠个人才智和奋斗一定能获得财富和理想中的幸福。在军队服役期间，他爱上了富家女黛西，在他眼里，她的美貌和她所代表的生活方式就是他梦寐以求的理想化身。但他的身份地位是黛西的家庭不可能接受的。他们分手后，黛西嫁给了汤姆。盖茨比经过几年卧薪尝胆，从身无分文到富甲一方，他的成功一方面通过不择手段的非法经营，另一方面靠的是他对爱情理想始终不渝的信念。当他能够用金钱买到进入上流社会的入场券后，他在自己的豪宅中不断举行宴会，希望吸引黛西与他重温旧梦，重新得到黛西和理想中的爱情，让时光倒转。然而，他心目中的黛西只是他自己创造的梦幻，现实中的黛西却和她的阶层中的其他人一样浅薄，不会为盖茨比心中的爱情理想而放弃自己浑浑噩噩但优雅安定的生活。黛西驾车撞死汤姆的情妇后，盖茨比为保护黛西而准备为此承担责任，黛西却将他抛在一边和她丈夫一走了之。死者的丈夫误认为盖茨比是肇事凶手而将他枪杀。

赏　析

小说表面上是一个爱情故事，但实际上却是对社会现状的讽刺批判。它描述了当时寻欢作乐和价值沦丧的社会风气。比如，小说真实再现了盖茨比挥霍的晚会场面，客人们空虚无聊的生活方式，以及盖茨比经营非法买卖敛取财富的背景，这些都是这一时代的典型写照。而另一方面，自早期移民开始，美国人梦想在这片民主、平等、自由、富饶的土地上，通过个人奋斗获得财富、幸福和理想。但是物质富裕带来的却是精神堕落和理想的破灭，同时，财富的增加并没有消除社会贫困和社会各阶层的狭隘偏见。在盖茨比身上可以清楚看到美国式的理想和精神追求，他的“了不起”就在于他对理想的执着。的确，没有理想，人与行尸走肉无异，但他的理想在与时代现实的冲突中却又显得天真，虚幻。他将奋斗和生命的意义仅仅建立在理想化的黛西和她代表的财富之上，而当现实无情地将这个梦幻击碎后，他的奋斗和生命便丧失了存在的意义，他其实是被他自己的梦想所杀死的。

小说的结构和主题天然合一。小说突出比照了盖茨比与黛西夫妇和他们所代表的社会阶层各自不同的价值观。小说通过第一人称叙事者尼克的视角，在第一章就将两组人并列展示在读者面前。在前四章，通过故事结构安排使两组人交替登场，这一方法使读者能够客观比较两组人之间的差异。从第五章开始两组人的交往冲突交织发展，使两组人之间的差异在他们的交往中进一步明晰，直到他们之间的冲突将故事推向高潮，最终矛盾的解决以悲剧告终。同时，小说的叙述视角也起到了强化主题的作用。尼克作为旁观者出入于两组人的社会圈子，但他的生活方式又和他们完全不同，这样便造成读者与小说人物之间的离间效果，使读者能保持客观距离从整体上审视两组人的不同生活态度，而不必被细节过于分散注意力。而当尼克通过他的女友和盖茨比以各自不同的视角讲述盖茨比和黛西的恋情时（第四章，第八章），这一离间效果得到进一步强化，使读者从不同角度审视盖茨比所坚信的爱以及爱情的理想化成分和社会现实成分。

Great Gatsby

Chapter 9

After two years I remember the rest of that day, and that night and the next day, only as an endless drill of police and photographers and newspaper men in and out of Gatsby's front door. A rope stretched across the main gate and a policeman by it kept out the curious, but little boys soon discovered that they could enter through my yard and there were always a few of them clustered open-mouthed about the pool. Someone with a positive manner, perhaps a detective, used the expression "mad man" as he bent over Wilson's body that afternoon, and the adventitious authority of his voice set the key for the newspaper reports next morning.

Most of those reports were a nightmare—grotesque, circumstantial, eager and untrue. When Michaelis's[4] testimony at the inquest brought to light Wilson's suspicions of his wife I thought the whole tale would shortly be served up in racy pasquinade—but Catherine[5], who might have said anything, didn't say a word. She showed a surprising amount of character about it too—looked at the coroner with determined eyes under that corrected brow of hers and swore that her sister had never seen Gatsby, that her sister was completely happy with her husband, that her sister had been into no mischief whatever. She convinced herself of it and cried into her handkerchief as if the very suggestion was more than she could endure. So Wilson was reduced to a man "deranged by grief" in order that the case might remain in its simplest form. And it rested there.

But all this part of it seemed remote and unessential. I found myself on Gatsby's side, and alone. From the moment I telephoned news of the catastrophe to West Egg village[6], every surmise about him, and every practical question, was referred to me. At first I was surprised and confused; then, as he lay in his house and didn't move or breathe or speak hour upon hour it grew upon me that I was responsible, because no one else was interested—interested, I mean, with that intense personal interest to which every one has some vague right at the end.

I called up Daisy[7] half an hour after we found him, called her instinctively and without hesitation. But she and Tom[8] had gone away early that afternoon, and taken baggage with them.

"Left no address?"

"No."

"Say when they'd be back?"

"No."

"Any idea where they are? How I could reach them?"

"I don't know. Can't say."

I wanted to get somebody for him. I wanted to go into the room where he lay and reassure him: "I'll get somebody for you, Gatsby. Don't worry. Just trust me and I'll get somebody for you—"

Meyer Wolfshiem's[9] name wasn't in the phone book. The butler gave me his office address on Broadway and I called Information, but by the time I had the number it was long after five and no one answered the phone.

"Will you ring again?"

"I've rung them three times."

"It's very important."

"Sorry. I'm afraid no one's there."

I went back to the drawing room and thought for an instant that they were chance visitors, all these official people who suddenly filled it. But as they drew back the sheet and looked at Gatsby with unmoved eyes, his protest continued in my brain.

"Look here, old sport, you've got to get somebody for me. You've got to try hard. I can't go through this alone."

Some one started to ask me questions but I broke away and going upstairs looked hastily through the unlocked parts of his desk—he'd never told me definitely that his parents were dead. But there was nothing—only the picture of Dan Cody[10], a token of forgotten violence staring down from the wall.

Next morning I sent the butler to New York with a letter to Wolfsheim which asked for information and urged him to come out on the next train. That request seemed superfluous when I wrote it. I was sure he'd start when he saw the newspapers, just as I was sure there'd be a wire from Daisy before noon—but neither a wire nor Mr. Wolfsheim arrived, no one arrived except more police and photographers and newspaper men.When the butler brought back Wolfsheim's answer I began to have a feeling of defiance, of scornful solidarity between Gatsby and me against them all.

Dear Mr. Carraway.

This has been one of the most terrible shocks of my life to me I hardly can believe it that it is true at all. Such a mad act as that man did should make us all think. I cannot come down now as I am tied up in some very important business and cannot get mixed up in this thing now. If there is anything I can do a little later let me know in a letter by Edgar. I hardly know where I am when I hear about a thing like this and am completely knocked down and out.

Yours truly

MEYER WOLFSHIEM

and then hasty addenda beneath:

Let me know about the funeral etc do not know his family at all.

When the phone rang that afternoon and Long Distance said Chicago was calling I thought this would be Daisy at last. But the connection came through as a man's voice, very thin and far way.

"This is Slagle[11] speaking..."

"Yes?" The name was unfamiliar.

"Hell of a note, isn't it? Get my wire?"

"There haven't been any wires."

"Young Parke's[12] in trouble," he said rapidly. "They picked him up[13] when he handed the bonds over the counter. They got a circular from New York giving'em the numbers just five minutes before. What d'you know about that, hey? You never can tell in these hick towns—"

"Hello!" I interrupted breathlessly. "Look here—this isn't Mr. Gatsby.

Mr. Gatsby's dead."

There was a long silence on the other end of the wire, followed by an exclamation... then a quick squawk as the connection was broken.

I think it was on the third day that a telegram signed Henry C. Gatz arrived from a town in Minnesota. It said only that the sender was leaving immediately and to postpone the funeral until he came.

It was Gatsby's father, a solemn old man very helpless and dismayed, bundled up in a long cheap ulster against the warm September day. His eyes leaked continuously with excitement and when I took the bag and umbrella from his hands he began to pull so incessantly at his sparse grey beard that I had difficulty in getting off his coat. He was on the point of collapse so I took him into the music room and made him sit down while I sent for something to eat. But he wouldn't eat and the glass of milk spilled from his trembling hand.

"I saw it in the Chicago newspaper," he said. "It was all in the Chicago newspaper. I started right away."

"I didn't know how to reach you."

His eyes, seeing nothing, moved ceaselessly about the room.

"It was a mad man," he said. "He must have been mad."

"Wouldn't you like some coffee?" I urged him.

"I don't want anything. I'm all right now, Mr.—"

"Carraway."

"Well, I'm all right now. Where have they got Jimmy?"

I took him into the drawing-room, where his son lay, and left him there. Some little boys had come up on the steps and were looking into the hall; when I told them who had arrived they went reluctantly away.

After a little while Mr. Gatz opened the door and came out, his mouth ajar, his face flushed slightly, his eyes leaking isolated and unpunctual tears. He had reached an age where death no longer has the quality of ghastly surprise, and when he looked around him now for the first time and saw the height and splendor of the hall and the great rooms opening out from it into other rooms his grief began to be mixed with an awed pride. I helped him to a bedroom upstairs; while he took off his coat and vest I told him that all arrangements had been deferred until he came.

"I didn't know what you'd want, Mr. Gatsby—"

"Gatz is my name."

"—Mr. Gatz. I thought you might want to take the body west."

He shook his head.

"Jimmy always liked it better down East. He rose up to his position in the East. Were you a friend of my boy's, Mr.—?"

"We were close friends."

"He had a big future before him, you know. He was only a young man but he had a lot of brain power here."

He touched his head impressively and I nodded.

"If he'd of lived he'd of been a great man[14]. A man like James J. Hill[15]. He'd of helped build up the country."

"That's true," I said, uncomfortably.

He fumbled at the embroidered coverlet, trying to take it from the bed, and lay down stiffly—was instantly asleep.

That night an obviously frightened person called up and demanded to know who I was before he would give his name.

"This is Mr. Carraway," I said.

"Oh—" He sounded relieved. "This is Klipspringer[16]."

I was relieved too for that seemed to promise another friend at Gatsby's grave. I didn't want it to be in the papers and draw a sightseeing crowd so I'd been calling up a few people myself.They were hard to find.

"The funeral's tomorrow," I said. "Three o'clock, here at the house.I wish you'd tell anybody who'd be interested."

"Oh, I will," he broke out hastily. "Of course I'm not likely to see anybody, but if I do."

His tone made me suspicious.

"Of course you'll be there yourself."

"Well, I'll certainly try. What I called about is—"

"Wait a minute," I interrupted. "How about saying you'll come?"

"Well, the fact is—the truth of the matter is that I'm staying with some people up here in Greenwich[17] and they rather expect me to be with them tomorrow. In fact there's a sort of picnic or something.Of course I' up ll do my very best to get away."

I ejaculated an unrestrained "Huh!" and he must have heard me for he went on nervously:

"What I called up about was a pair of shoes I left there. I wonder if it'd be too much trouble to have the butler send them on. You see they're tennis shoes and I'm sort of helpless without them. My address is care of B. F.—"

I didn't hear the rest of the name because I hung up the receiver.

After that I felt a certain shame for Gatsby—one gentleman to whom I telephoned implied that he had got what he deserved. However, that was my fault, for he was one of those who used to sneer most bitterly at Gatsby on the courage of Gatsby's liquor and I should have known better than to call him.

The morning of the funeral I went up to New York to see Meyer Wolfshiem; I couldn't seem to reach him any other way. The door that I pushed open on the advice of an elevator boy was marked "The Swastika Holding Company" and at first there didn't seem to be any one inside.But when I'd shouted "Hello" several times in vain an argument broke out behind a partition and presently a lovely Jewess appeared at an interior door and scrutinized me with black hostile eyes.

"Nobody's in," she said. "Mr. Wolfshiem's gone to Chicago."

The first part of this was obviously untrue for someone had begun to whistle "The Rosary," tunelessly, inside.

"Please say that Mr. Carraway wants to see him."

"I can't get him back from Chicago, can I?"

At this moment a voice, unmistakably Wolfshiem's called "Stella!" from the other side of the door.

"Leave your name on the desk," she said quickly. "I'll give it to him when he gets back."

"But I know he's there."

She took a step toward me and began to slide her hands indignantly up and down her hips.

"You young men think you can force your way in here any time," she scolded. "We're getting sickantired18 of it. When I say he's in Chicago, he's in ChiCAgo."

I mentioned Gatsby.

"Oh—h!" She looked at me over again. "Will you just—what was your name?"

She vanished. In a moment Meyer Wolfshiem stood solemnly in the doorway, holding out both hands. He drew me into his office, remarking in a reverent voice that it was a sad time for all of us, and offered me a cigar.

"My memory goes back to when I first met him," he said. "A young major just out of the army and covered over with medals he got in the war. He was so hard up he had to keep on wearing his uniform because he couldn't buy some regular clothes. First time I saw him was when he come[19] into Winebrenner's poolroom at Forty-third Street and asked for a job. He hadn't eat anything[20] for a couple of days. 'Come on have some lunch with me,' I sid[21]. He ate more than four dollars' worth of food in half an hour."

"Did you start him in business?" I inquired.

"Start him! I made him."

"Oh."

"I raised him up out of nothing, right out of the gutter. I saw right away he was a fine appearing, gentlemanly young man, and when he told me he was an Oggsford[22] I knew I could use him good. I got him to join up in the American Legion[23] and he used to stand high there. Right off he did some work for a client of mine up to Albany. We were so thick like that in everything—" He held up two bulbous fingers "—always together."

I wondered if this partnership had included the World's Series transaction[24] in 1919.

"Now he's dead," I said after a moment. "You were his closest friend, so I know you'll want to come to his funeral this afternoon."

"I'd like to come."

"Well, come then."

The hair in his nostrils quivered slightly and as he shook his head his eyes filled with tears.

"I can't do it—I can't get mixed up in it," he said.

"There's nothing to get mixed up in. It's all over now."

"When a man gets killed I never like to get mixed up in it in any way. I keep out. When I was a young man it was different—if a friend of mine died, no matter how, I stuck with them to the end. You may think that's sentimental but I mean it—to the bitter end."

I saw that for some reason of his own he was determined not to come, so I stood up.

"Are you a college man? " He inquired suddenly.

For a moment I thought he was going to suggest a "gonnegtion[25]" but he only nodded and shook my hand.

"Let us learn to show our friendship for a man when he is alive and not after he is dead," he suggested. "After that my own rule is to let everything alone."

When I left his office the sky had turned dark and I got back to West Egg in a drizzle. After changing my clothes I went next door and found Mr. Gatz walking up and down excitedly in the hall. His pride in his son and in his son's possessions was continually increasing and now he had something to show me.

"Jimmy sent me this picture." He took out his wallet with trembling fingers.

"Look there."

It was a photograph of the house, cracked in the corners and dirty with many hands. He pointed out every detail to me eagerly. "Look there!" and then sought admiration from my eyes. He had shown it so often that I think it was more real to him now than the house itself.

"Jimmy sent it to me. I think it's a very pretty picture. It shows up well."

"Very well. Had you seen him lately?"

"He come out[26] to see me two years ago and bought me the house I live in now. Of course we was broke up when he run off[27] from home but I see now there was a reason for it. He knew he had a big future in front of him. And ever since he made a success he was very generous with me. "

He seemed reluctant to put away the picture, held it for another minute, lingeringly, before my eyes. Then he returned the wallet and pulled from his pocket a ragged old copy of a book called *Hopalong Cassidy*.

"Look here, this is a book he had when he was a boy. It just shows you."

He opened it at the back cover and turned it around for me to see.

On the last fly-leaf was printed the word SCHEDULE, and the date September 12th, 1906. And underneath:

Rise from bed................ 6.00 A.M.

Dumbbell exercise and wall-scaling...... 6.15-6.30 ...

Study electricity, etc............ 7.15-8.15 ...

Work..................... 8.30-4.30 P.M.

Baseball and sports............. 4.30-5.00 ...

Practice elocution, poise and how to attain it 5.00-6.00 ...

Study needed inventions........... 7.00-9.00 ...

GENERAL RESOLVES

No wasting time at Shafters or a name, indecipherable

No more smokeing or chewing

Bath every other day

Read one improving book or magazine per week

Save $5.00 [crossed out] $3.00 per week

Be better to parents

"I come across this book[28] by accident," said the old man. "It just shows you, don't it?[29]"

"It just shows you."

"Jimmy was bound to get ahead. He always had some resolves like this or something. Do you notice what he's got about improving his mind? He was always great for that. He told me I et like a hog[30] once and I beat him for it."

He was reluctant to close the book, reading each item aloud and then looking eagerly at me. I think he rather expected me to copy down the list for my own use.

A little before three the Lutheran minister arrived from Flushing and I began to look involuntarily out the windows for other cars. So did Gatsby's father. And as the time passed and the servants came in and stood waiting in the hall, his eyes began to blink anxiously and he spoke of the rain in a worried uncertain way. The minister glanced several times at his watch so I took him aside and asked him to wait for half an hour. But it wasn't any use. Nobody came.

About five o'clock our procession of three cars reached the cemetery and stopped in a thick drizzle beside the gate—first a motor hearse, horribly black and wet, then Mr. Gatz and the minister and I in the limousine, and, a little later, four or five servants and the postman from West Egg in Gatsby's station wagon, all wet to the skin. As we started through the gate into the cemetery I heard a car stop and then the sound of someone splashing after us over the soggy ground. I looked around. It was the man with owl-eyed glasses[31] whom I had found marvelling over Gatsby's books in the library one night three months before.

I'd never seen him since then. I don't know how he knew about the funeral or even his name. The rain poured down his thick glasses and he took them off and wiped them to see the protecting canvas unrolled from Gatsby's grave.

I tried to think about Gatsby then for a moment but he was already too far away and I could only remember, without resentment, that Daisy hadn't sent a message or a flower. Dimly I heard someone murmur "Blessed are the dead that the rain falls on," and then the owl-eyed man said "Amen to that," in a brave voice.

We straggled down quickly through the rain to the cars. Owl-Eyes spoke to me by the gate.

"I couldn't get to the house," he remarked.

"Neither could anybody else."

"Go on!" He started. "Why, my God! they used to go there by the hundreds."

He took off his glasses and wiped them again outside and in.

"The poor son-of-a-bitch," he said.

One of my most vivid memories is of coming back west from prep school and later from college at Christmas time. Those who went farther than Chicago would gather in the old dim Union Station at six o'clock of a December evening with a few Chicago friends already caught up into their own holiday gayeties to bid them a hasty goodbye. I remember the fur coats of the girls returning from Miss This or That's and the chatter of frozen breath and the hands waving overhead as we caught sight of old acquaintances and the matchings of invitations: "Are you going to the Ordways'? the Herseys'? the Schultzes'?" and the long green tickets clasped tight in our gloved hands. And last the murky yellow cars of the Chicago, Milwaukee and St. Paul Railroad looking cheerful as Christmas itself on the tracks beside the gate.

When we pulled out into the winter night and the real snow, our snow, began to stretch out beside us and twinkle against the windows, and the dim lights of small Wisconsin stations moved by, a sharp wild brace came suddenly into the air. We drew in deep breaths of it as we walked back from dinner through the cold vestibules, unutterably aware of our identity with this country for one strange hour before we melted indistinguishably into it again.

That's my middle west—not the wheat or the prairies or the lost Swede towns but the thrilling, returning trains of my youth and the street lamps and sleigh bells in the frosty dark and the shadows of holly wreaths thrown by lighted windows on the snow. I am part of that, a little solemn with the feel of those long winters, a little complacent from growing up in the Carraway house in a city where dwellings are still called through decades by a family's name. I see now that this has been a story of the West, after all—Tom and Gatsby, Daisy and Jordan[32] and I, were all Westerners, and perhaps we possessed some deficiency in common which made us subtly unadaptable to Eastern life.

Even when the East excited me most, even when I was most keenly aware of its superiority to the bored, sprawling, swollen towns beyond the Ohio[33], with their interminable inquisitions which spared only the children and the very old —even then it had always for me a quality of distortion. West Egg especially still figures in my more fantastic dreams. I see it as a night scene by El Greco[34]: a hundred houses, at once conventional and grotesque, crouching under a sullen, overhanging sky and a lustreless moon. In the foreground four solemn men in dress suits are walking along the sidewalk with a stretcher on which lies a drunken woman in a white evening dress. Her hand, which dangles over the side, sparkles cold with jewels. Gravely the men turn in at a house—the wrong house. But no one knows the woman's name, and no one cares.

After Gatsby's death the East was haunted for me like that, distorted beyond my eyes' power of correction. So when the blue smoke of brittle leaves was in the air and the wind blew the wet laundry stiff on the line I decided to come back home.

There was one thing to be done before I left, an awkward, unpleasant thing that perhaps had better have been let alone. But I wanted to leave things in order and not just trust that obliging and indifferent sea to sweep my refuse away. I saw Jordan Baker and talked over and around what had happened to us together and what had happened afterward to me, and she lay perfectly still listening in a big chair. She was dressed to play golf and I remember thinking she looked like a good illustration, her chin raised a little, jauntily, her hair the color of an autumn leaf, her face the same brown tint as the fingerless glove on her knee. When I had finished she told me without comment that she was engaged to another man. I doubted that though there were several she could have married at a nod of her head but I pretended to be surprised. For just a minute I wondered if I wasn't making a mistake, then I thought it all over again quickly and got up to say good-bye.

"Nevertheless you did throw me over," said Jordan suddenly. "You threw me over on the telephone. I don't give a damn about you now but it was a new experience for me and I felt a little dizzy for a while."

We shook hands.

"Oh, and do you remember—" she added, "—a conversation we had once about driving a car?"

"Why—not exactly."

"You said a bad driver was only safe until she met another bad driver? Well, I met another bad driver, didn't I? I mean it was careless of me to make such a wrong guess. I thought you were rather an honest, straightforward person. I thought it was your secret pride."

"I'm thirty," I said. "I'm five years too old to lie to myself and call it honor."

She didn't answer. Angry, and half in love with her, and tremendously sorry, I turned away.

One afternoon late in October I saw Tom Buchanan. He was walking ahead of me along Fifth Avenue in his alert, aggressive way, his hands out a little from his body as if to fight off interference, his head moving sharply here and there, adapting itself to his restless eyes. Just as I slowed up to avoid overtaking him he stopped and began frowning into the windows of a jewelry store. Suddenly he saw me and walked back holding out his hand.

"What's the matter, Nick? Do you object to shaking hands with me?"

"Yes. You know what I think of you."

"You're crazy, Nick," he said quickly. "Crazy as hell. I don't know what's the matter with you."

"Tom," I inquired, "what did you say to Wilson that afternoon?"

He stared at me without a word and I knew I had guessed right about those missing hours. I started to turn away but he took a step after me and grabbed my arm.

"I told him the truth," he said. "He came to the door while we were getting ready to leave and when I sent down word that we weren't in he tried to force his way upstairs. He was crazy enough to kill me if I hadn't told him who owned the car. His hand was on a revolver in his pocket every minute he was in the house—" He broke off defiantly. "What if I did tell him? That fellow had it coming to him. He threw dust into your eyes just like he did in Daisy's but he was a tough one. He ran over Myrtle like you'd run over a dog and never even stopped his car."

There was nothing I could say, except the one unutterable fact that it wasn't true.

"And if you think I didn't have my share of suffering—look here, when I went to give up that flat and saw that damn box of dog biscuits sitting there on the sideboard I sat down and cried like a baby. By God it was awful—"

I couldn't forgive him or like him but I saw that what he had done was, to him, entirely justified. It was all very careless and confused. They were careless people, Tom and Daisy—they smashed up things and creatures and then retreated back into their money or their vast carelessness or whatever it was that kept them together, and let other people clean up the mess they had made...

I shook hands with him; it seemed silly not to, for I felt suddenly as though I were talking to a child. Then he went into the jewelry store to buy a pearl necklace—or perhaps only a pair of cuff buttons—rid of my provincial squeamishness forever.

Gatsby's house was still empty when I left—the grass on his lawn had grown as long as mine. One of the taxi drivers in the village never took a fare past the entrance gate without stopping for a minute and pointing inside; perhaps it was he who drove Daisy and Gatsby over to East Egg[35] the night of the accident and perhaps he had made a story about it all his own. I didn't want to hear it and I avoided him when I got off the train.

I spent my Saturday nights in New York because those gleaming, dazzling parties of his were with me so vividly that I could still hear the music and the laughter faint and incessant from his garden and the cars going up and down his drive. One night I did hear a material car[36] there and saw its lights stop at his front steps. But I didn't investigate. Probably it was some final guest who had been away at the ends of the earth and didn't know that the party was over.

On the last night, with my trunk packed and my car sold to the grocer, I went over and looked at that huge incoherent failure of a house once more. On the white steps an obscene word, scrawled by some boy with a piece of brick, stood out clearly in the moonlight and I erased it, drawing my shoe raspingly along the stone. Then I wandered down to the beach and sprawled out on the sand.

Most of the big shore places were closed now and there were hardly any lights except the shadowy, moving glow of a ferryboat across the Sound[37].And as the moon rose higher the inessential houses began to melt away until gradually I became aware of the old island38 here that flowered once for Dutch sailors' eyes—a fresh, green breast of the new world. Its vanished trees, the trees that had made way for Gatsby's house, had once pandered in whispers to the last and greatest of all human dreams; for a transitory enchanted moment man must have held his breath in the presence of this continent, compelled into an aesthetic contemplation he neither understood nor desired, face to face for the last time in history with something commensurate to his capacity for wonder.

And as I sat there brooding on the old, unknown world, I thought of Gatsby's wonder when he first picked out the green light[39] at the end of Daisy's dock[40]. He had come a long way to this blue lawn and his dream must have seemed so close that he could hardly fail to grasp it. He did not know that it was already behind him, somewhere back in that vast obscurity beyond the city, where the dark fields of the republic rolled on under the night.

Gatsby believed in the green light, the orgastic future that year by year recedes before us. It eluded us then, but that's no matter—tomorrow we will run faster, stretch out our arms farther... And one fine morning—So we beat on, boats against the current, borne back ceaselessly into the past.

Questions:

1. Do you think Gatsby deserves to be called "the great" ? Why?
2. Does "the green light" Gatsby believed in exist in reality? Why or why not?
3. What does Gatsby's Schedule reveal about him and hoe does it relate to the American Dream?
4. When you read this line "He (the man with owl-eyed glasses) took off his glasses and wiped them again, outside and in ," what image does it create in your mind , given the novel's numerous references to the strikingly strange scene of the spectacled eyes?

注　释

1. 见海明威一节注释1.
2. I: 故事叙述人尼克(Nick Carraway).

3. Wilson：(George·B·Wilson)威尔逊是汤姆情妇的丈夫。黛西驾车时将他妻子撞死。他误以为是盖茨比将他妻子撞死，在枪杀盖茨比后自杀(详见第二章、第七章和第八章)。

4. Michaelis：咖啡店店主，汽车肇事时他在现场，但连汽车的颜色都没有看清(第七章)。

5. Catherine：车祸受害者(Myrtle)的妹妹(第二章)。

6. West Egg Village：西卵镇。小说主人公盖茨比(Jay Gatzby)和故事叙述者尼克居住的地方。

7. Daisy：(Daisy Buchanan)黛西，曾经是盖茨比的情人，后嫁给了汤姆(第一章)。

8. Tom：(Tom Buchanan)汤姆(第一章)。

9. Meyer Wolfsheim：非法操纵比赛的赌徒，盖茨比做非法生意的伙伴(第四章)。

10. Dan Cody：曾在西部内华达州开银矿发迹，盖茨比年轻时遇见他并为他工作(第六章)。

11. Slagle：盖茨比做非法生意的伙伴。

12. Parke：盖茨比做非法生意的伙伴。

13. They picked him up...：他们把他逮捕了。这证实了盖茨比参与了非法生意。

14. If he'd of lived, he'd of been a great man.：If he'd lived, he'd have been a great man.

15. James J.Hill：詹姆斯·J. 希尔(1838—1916)，美国金融家和铁路建筑家。

16. Klipspringer：一个经常寄宿在盖茨比家的人(第四章)。

17. Greenwich：格林威治，美国康涅狄格州西南部城镇。

18. Sickantired：sick and tired

19. He come：he came

20. He hadn't eat anything：he hadn't eaten anything

21. I sid：I said

22. Oggsford：Oxford

23. American Legion：美国军团（美国退伍军人组织）。
24. World Series transaction：World Series，世界系列赛（美国棒球系列比赛）；transaction：这里指操纵比赛的非法交易。
25. Gonnegtion：connection
26. He come out：He came out
27. we was broke up when he run off：we broke up when he ran off.
28. I come across this book：I came across this book.
29. it just shows you，don't it? it just shows you，doesn't it?
30. I et like a hog：I ate like a hog.
31. the man with owl-eye glasses：盖茨比宴会上的的客人（第三章）。小说中有一些独特的眼睛形象，如眼镜广告牌上巨大的埃克尔伯格医生（Dr. Eckleburg）的眼睛透过黄色眼镜注视灰暗的世界。这些眼睛形象使读者联想到盖茨比对世界的错误看法，他完全被虚幻的理想蒙住了视线，看不清真实的世界，而与此形成对照的是黛西夫妇，他们的眼睛却只能看见物质的世界。他们各自的视线都是扭曲的。
32. Jordan（Jordan Baker）：乔丹，高尔夫球运动员，曾与尼克有恋爱关系（第一章）。
33. the Ohio = the Ohio River：美国中东部主要河流。
34. a night scene by EI Greco：EI Greco（1541—1614，西班牙画家。这里尼克以画中变形了的景物暗喻东部地区的扭曲的生活方式。
35. East Egg：东卵镇，黛西夫妇居住的富人区。
36. a material car：真实的而不是幻觉中的汽车。
37. the Sound：Long Island Sound：长岛海峡。
38. the old island：Long Island
39. green light：绿色在英语里象征青春和生命。西方文化传说中光明与黑暗往往有不同的象征意义：如，善与恶，愚昧与知识等。书中多次提到盖茨比对绿色光明的向往（第一章），他以为黛西就是他向往的光明。
40. Daisy's dock：这里既指黛西住所外码头上的指示灯（其实你应该是红色），

又指盖茨比心中理想的停泊港湾。

You don't write because you want to say something, you write becaue you've got something to say.

An author ought to write for the youth of his own generation, the critics of the next, and the schoolmasters of ever after.

—F'Scott Fitzgerald

第八章
威廉·福克纳 William Faulkner

作者简介

威廉·福克纳（William Faulkner，1897—1962），小说家。生于密西西比州新奥尔巴尼一没落贵族家庭，后随家迁居奥克斯福。中学时迷上诗歌，经常逃课，于最后一年辍学。在就读于耶鲁大学的好友斯东（Phil Stone）的指点下，继续广泛阅读文学名著。1918年，女友奥昙（Estelle Oldham）与别人订婚后，参加英国皇家空军赴加拿大受训，因一战结束而没上前线。退伍后在密西西比大学学习一年并开始发表诗作。1924年，出版第一部诗集《大理石牧神》（The Marble Faun）后，动身经新奥尔良赴欧洲旅行。在新奥尔良结识安德森（Sherwood Anderson），并经他帮助发表了第一部小说《士兵的报酬》（*Soldier's Pay*，1926）。安德森建议他着力用小说体裁写他家乡的素材，发展自己的风格，所以他在发表了描写艺术家的《蚊群》（*Mosquitoes*，1927）后，便根据家乡情景虚构出约克纳帕塔法县，开始创作以内战后南方的物质与精神衰败的约克纳帕塔法系列小说，其中主要作品有《喧哗与骚动》（*The Sound and the Fury*，1929）、《我弥留之际》（*As I Lay Dying*，1930）《八月之光》（*Light in August*，1932）、《押沙龙，押沙龙！》（*Absalom, Absalom!* 1936）等。这些作品创造性地运用了意识流与多视角等叙事手法，具有复杂的结构和史诗的风格。他名下共有23部长篇小说、11个短篇小说集、7个诗集、6个电影剧本、一个电视剧剧本。他获得的大奖有1949年度诺贝尔文学奖、1954和1962年度普利策奖等。

赏 析

《烧牲口棚》写于福克纳创作鼎盛期中的1938年，1939年作为该年度美国最佳短篇小说而获首届“欧·亨利纪念奖”，一直被视为福克纳最具代表性的短篇小说之一。

南方贫穷白人的生活是福克纳较为关注的题材。斯诺普斯（Snopes）这一贫穷白人家族的故事在他的《沙多里斯》（*Sartoris*, 1929）、《村子》（*The Hamlet*, 1940）、《小镇》（*The Town*, 1957）、《大宅》（*The Mansion*, 1959）等长篇小说中得到集中描写。《烧牲口棚》也强调了穷苦白人与庄园主之间的激烈冲突。阿伯纳（Abner）擅入德斯潘的大宅、糟蹋他的地毯、烧他的牲口棚等行为，都明确表现了阿伯纳对庄园主的仇视态度，以及他誓死维护自己的尊严的意志。小说写了阿伯纳的贫困和他不屈不挠的斗争精神，反映了作者对他的同情，但也写了使他众叛亲离、自取灭亡的偏执与暴烈，传达出作者对他的责备。

处于痛苦的成长期的男孩也是福克纳所感兴趣的。在《烧牲口棚》中，萨蒂（Sarty）的痛苦不仅在于他必须承受过去的罪孽所产生的后果，比如在哈里斯（Harris）的牲口棚被烧后，他被骂作“牲口棚纵火犯”，并被打得头破血流，还在于他必须做出十分艰难的选择：是按父亲阿伯纳的要求忠实于自己的血统，从而继续生活在“恐惧与绝望”之中，还是背叛血统去追求德斯潘“漂亮、雪白”“像法院一般”的大宅所象征的“和平与快乐”。萨蒂的最后选择无疑为他的追求创造了机会。但他天真，没有像阿伯纳那样认识到德斯潘的大宅建在黑人和白人的汗水之上，这又难免让人对他的未来感到担忧。萨蒂在福克纳的作品中没有再出现过。

萨蒂当时没有认识到的还有阿伯纳为什么只生小火取暖，阿伯纳在内战中的真实表现等。而读者则可从叙事者的有关叙述中了解到他的这种幼稚以及他所不了解的其他情况。小说叙事者具有传统的第三人称叙事中的全知视点，但他的叙述具有高度的选择性，主要选择叙述萨蒂所能看到、感到、想到的东西，使得叙述客观而又简洁。然而叙事者有时也站出来发表年幼的主人公尚不具备的洞见，从而加强了他可悲处境的感染力和他成熟过程的戏剧性。

Barn Burning

The store in which the justice of the Peace's court was sitting smelled of cheese. The boy, crouched on his nail keg at the back of the crowded room, knew he smelled cheese, and more: from where he sat he could see the ranked shelves close-packed with the solid, squat, dynamic shapes of tin cans whose labels his stomach read, not from the lettering which meant nothing to his mind but from the scarlet devils and the silver curve of fish-this, the cheese which he knew he smelled and the hermetic meat[1] which his intestines believed he smelled coming in intermittent gusts momentary and brief between the other constant one, the smell and sense just a little of fear because mostly of despair and grief, the old fierce pull of blood. He could not see the table where the Justice sat and before which his father and his father's enemy (our enemy he thought in that despair; ourn! mine and hisn both! He's my father!) stood, but he could hear them, the two of them that is, because his father had said no word yet:

"But what proof have you, Mr. Harris?"

"I told you. The hog got into my corn. I caught it up and sent it back to him. He had no fence that would hold it. I told him so, warned him. The next time I put the hog in my pen. When he came to get it I gave him enough wire to patch up his pen. The next time I put the hog up and kept it. I rode down to his house and saw the wire I gave him still rolled on to the spool in his yard. I told him he could have the hog when he paid me a dollar pound fee. That evening a nigger came with the dollar and got the hog. He was a strange nigger. He said, 'He say to tell you wood and hay kin burn.' I said, 'What?' 'That whut he say to tell you,' the nigger said. 'Wood and hay kin burn.' That night my barn burned. I got the stock out but I lost the barn."

"Where is the nigger? Have you got him?"

"It was a strange nigger, I tell you. I don't know what became of him."

"But that's not proof. Don't you see that's not proof?"

"Get that boy up here. He knows." For a moment the boy thought too that the man meant his older brother until Harris said, "Not him. The little one. The boy," and, crouching, small for his age, small and wiry like his father, in patched and faded jeans even too small for him, with straight, uncombed, brown hair and eyes gray and wild as storm scud, he saw the men between himself and the table part and become a lane of grim faces, at the end of which he saw the justice, a shabby, collarless, graying man in spectacles, beckoning him. He felt no floor under his bare feet; he seemed to walk beneath the palpable weight of the grim turning faces. His father, stiff in his black Sunday coat donned not for the trial but for the moving, did not even look at him. He aims for me to lie, he thought, again with that frantic grief and despair. And I will have to do hit.

"What's your name, boy?" the justice said.

"Colonel Sartoris[2] Snopes," the boy whispered.

"Hey?" the Justice said. "Talk louder. Colonel Sartoris? I reckon anybody named for Colonel Sartoris in this country can't help but tell the truth, can they?" The boy said nothing. Enemy! Enemy! he thought; for a moment he could not even see, could not see that the justice's face was kindly nor discern that his voice was troubled when he spoke to the man named Harris: "Do you want me to question this boy?" But he could hear, and during those subsequent long seconds while there was absolutely no sound in the crowded little room save that of quiet and intent breathing it was as if he had swung outward at the end of a grape vine, over a ravine, and at the top of the swing had been caught in a prolonged instant of mesmerized gravity, weightless in time.

"No!" Harris said violently, explosively. "Damnation! Send him out of here!" Now time, the fluid world, rushed beneath him again, the voices coming to him again through the smell of cheese and sealed meat, the fear and despair and the old grief of blood:

"This case is closed. I can't find against you, Snopes, but I can give you advice. Leave this country and don't come back to it."

His father spoke for the first time, his voice cold and harsh, level, without emphasis: "I aim to. I don't figure to stay in a country among people who..." he said something unprintable and vile, addressed to no one.

"That'll do," the Justice said. "Take your wagon and get out of this country before dark. Case dismissed."

His father turned, and he followed the stiff black coat, the wiry figure walking a little stiffly from where a Confederate provost's man's[3] musket ball had taken him in the heel on a stolen horse thirty years ago, followed the two backs now, since between the two lines of grim-faced men and out of the store and across the worn gallery and down the sagging steps and among the dogs and half-grown boys in the mild May dust, where as he passed a voice hissed:

"Barn burner!"

Again he could not see, whirling; there was a face in a red haze, moonlike, bigger than the full moon, the owner of it half again his size, he leaping in the red haze toward the face, feeling no blow, feeling no shock when his head struck the earth, scrabbling up and leaping again, feeling no blow this time either and tasting no blood, scrabbling up to see the other boy in full flight and himself already leaping into pursuit as his father's hand jerked him back, the harsh, cold voice speaking above him: "Go get in the wagon."

It stood in a grove of locusts and mulberries across the road. His two hulking sisters in their Sunday dresses and his mother and her sister in calico and sunbonnets were already in it, sitting on and among the sorry residue of the dozen and more movings which even the boy could remember the battered stove, the broken beds and chairs, the clock inlaid with mother-of-pearl, which would not run, stopped at some fourteen minutes past two o'clock of a dead and forgotten day and time, which had been his mother's dowry. She was crying, though when she saw him she drew her sleeve across her face and began to descend from the wagon. "Get back," the father said.

"He's hurt. I got to get some water and wash his..."

"Get back in the wagon," his father said. He got in too, over the tail-gate. His father mounted to the seat where the older brother already sat and struck the gaunt mules two savage blows with the peeled willow, but without heat. It was not even sadistic; it was exactly that same quality which in later years would cause his descendants to over-run the engine before putting a motor car into motion, striking and reining back in the same movement. The wagon went on, the store with its quiet crowd of grimly watching men dropped behind; a curve in the road hid it. Forever he thought. Maybe he's done satisfied now, now that he has... stopping himself, not to say it aloud even to himself. His mother's hand touched his shoulder.

"Does hit hurt?" she said.

"Naw," he said. "Hit don't hurt. Lemme be."

"Can't you wipe some of the blood off before hit dries?"

"I'll wash to-night," he said. "Lemme be, I tell you."

The wagon went on. He did not know where they were going. None of them ever did or ever asked, because it was always somewhere, always a house of sorts waiting for them a day or two days or even three days away. Likely his father had already arranged to make a crop on another farm before he... Again he had to stop himself. He (the father) always did. There was something about his wolflike independence and even courage when the advantage was at least neutral which impressed strangers, as if they got from his latent ravening ferocity not so much a sense of dependability as a feeling that his ferocious conviction in the rightness of his own actions would be of advantage to all whose interest lay with his.

That night they camped in a grove of oaks and beeches where a spring ran. The nights were still cool and they had a fire against it, of a rail lifted from a nearby fence and cut into lengths—a small fire, neat, niggard almost, a shrewd fire; such fires were his father's habit and custom always, even in freezing weather. Older, the boy might have remarked this and wondered why not a big one; why should not a man who had not only seen the waste and extravagance of war, but who had in his blood an inherent voracious prodigality with material not his own, have burned everything in sight? Then he might have gone a step farther and thought that that was the reason: that niggard blaze was the living fruit of nights passed during those four years in the woods hiding from all men, blue or gray[4], with his strings of horses (captured horses, he called them). And older still, he might have divined the true reason: that the element of fire spoke to some deep mainspring of his father's being, as the element of steel or of powder spoke to other men, as the one weapon for the preservation of integrity, else breath were not worth the breathing, and hence to be regarded with respect and used with discretion.

But he did not think this now and he had seen those same niggard blazes all his life. He merely ate his supper beside it and was already half asleep over his iron plate when his father called him, and once more he followed the stiff back, the stiff and ruthless limp, up the slope and on to the starlit road where, turning, he could see his father against the stars but without face or depth—a shape black, flat, and bloodless as though cut from tin in the iron folds of the frockcoat which had not been made for him, the voice harsh like tin and without heat like tin:

"You were fixing to tell them. You would have told him." He didn't answer. His father struck him with the flat of his hand on the side of the head, hard but without heat, exactly as he had struck the two mules at the store, exactly as he would strike either of them with any stick in order to kill a horse fly, his voice still without heat or anger: "You're getting to be a man. You got to learn. You got to learn to stick to your own blood or you ain't going to have any blood to stick to you. Do you think either of them, any man there this morning would? Don't you know all they wanted was a chance to get at me because they knew I had them beat? Eh?" Later, twenty years later, he was to tell himself, "If I had said they wanted only truth, justice, he would have hit me again." But now he said nothing. He was not crying. He just stood there. "Answer me," his father said.

"Yes," he whispered. His father turned.

"Get on to bed. We'll be there to-morrow."

To-morrow they were there. In the early afternoon the wagon stopped before a paintless two-room house identical almost with the dozen others it had stopped before even in the boy's ten years, and again, as on the other dozen occasions, his mother and aunt got down and began to unload the wagon, although his two sisters and his father and brother had not moved.

"Likely hit ain't fitten for hawgs," one of the sisters said.

"Nevertheless, fit it will and you'll hog it and like it," his father said. "Get out of them chairs and help your Ma unload."

The two sisters got down, big, bovine, in a flutter of cheap ribbons; one of them drew from the jumbled wagon bed a battered lantern, the other a worn broom. His father handed the reins to the older son and began to climb stiffly over the wheel. "When they get unloaded, take the team to the barn and feed them." Then he said, and at first the boy thought he was still speaking to his brother:

"Come with me."

"Me?" he said.

"Yes," his father said. "You."

"Abner," his mother said. His father paused and looked back—the harsh level stare beneath the shaggy, graying, irascible brows.

"I reckon I'll have a word with the man that aims to begin tomorrow owning me body and soul for the next eight months."

They went back up the road. A week ago—or before last night, that is—he would have asked where they were going, but not now. His father had struck him before last night but never before had he paused afterward to explain why; it was as if the blow and the following calm, outrageous voice still rang, repercussed, divulging nothing to him save the terrible handicap of being young, the light weight of his few years, just heavy enough to prevent his soaring free of the world as it seemed to be ordered but not heavy enough to keep him footed solid in it, to resist it and try to change the course of its events.

Presently he could see the grove of oaks and cedars and the other flowering trees and shrubs where the house would be, though not the house yet. They walked beside a fence massed with honeysuckle and Cherokee roses and came to a gate swinging open between two brick pillars, and now, beyond a sweep of drive, he saw the house for the first time and at that instant he forgot his father and the terror and despair both, and even when he remembered his father again (who had not stopped) the terror and despair did not return. Because, for all the twelve movings, they had sojourned until now in a poor country, a land of small farms and fields and houses, and he had never seen a house like this before. Hit's big as a courthouse he thought quietly, with a surge of peace and joy whose reason he could not have thought into words, being too young for that: They are safe from him. People whose lives are a part of this peace and dignity are beyond his touch, he no more to them than a buzzing wasp: capable of stinging for a little moment but that's all; the spell of this peace and dignity rendering even the barns and stable and cribs which belong to it impervious to the puny flames he might contrive... this, the peace and joy, ebbing for an instant as he looked again at the stiff black back, the stiff and implacable limp of the figure which was not dwarfed by the house, for the reason that it had never looked big anywhere and which now, against the serene columned backdrop, had more than ever that impervious quality of something cut ruthlessly from tin, depthless, as though, sidewise to the sun, it would cast no shadow. Watching him, the boy remarked the absolutely undeviating course which his father held and saw the stiff foot come squarely down in a pile of fresh droppings where a horse had stood in the drive and which his father could have avoided by a simple change of stride. But it ebbed only for a moment, though he could not have thought this into words either, walking on in the spell of the house, which he could even want but without envy, without sorrow, certainly never with that ravening and jealous rage which unknown to him walked in the iron like black coat before him. Maybe he will feel it too. Maybe it will even change him now from what maybe he couldn't help but be.

They crossed the portico. Now he could hear his father's stiff foot as it came down on the boards with clocklike finality, a sound out of all proportion to the displacement of the body it bore and which was not dwarfed either by the white door before it, as though it had attained to a sort of vicious and ravening minimum not to be dwarfed by anything—the flat, wide, black hat, the formal coat of broadcloth which had once been black but which had now the friction-glazed greenish cast of the bodies of old house flies, the lifted sleeve which was too large, the lifted hand like a curled claw. The door opened so promptly that the boy knew the Negro must have been watching them all the time, an old man with neat grizzled hair, in a linen jacket, who stood barring the door with his body, saying, "Wipe yo foots, white man, fo you come in here. Major ain't home nohow."

"Get out of my way, nigger," his father said, without heat too, flinging the door back and the Negro also and entering, his hat still on his head. And now the boy saw the prints of the stiff foot on the doorjamb and saw them appear on the pale rug behind the machinelike deliberation of the foot which seemed to bear (or transmit) twice the weight which the body compassed. The Negro was shouting "Miss Lula! Miss Lula!" somewhere behind them, then the boy, deluged as though by a warm wave by a suave turn of carpeted stair and a pendant glitter of chandeliers and a mute gleam of gold frames, heard the swift feet and saw her too, a lady—perhaps he had never seen her like before either—in a gray, smooth gown with lace at the throat and an apron tied at the waist and the sleeves turned back, wiping cake or biscuit dough from her hands with a towel as she came up the hall, looking not at his father at all but at the tracks on the blond rug with an expression of incredulous amazement.

"I tried," the Negro cried. "I tole him to..."

"Will you please go away?" she said in a shaking voice. "Major de Spain is not at home. Will you please go away?"

His father had not spoken again. He did not speak again. He did not even look at her. He just stood stiff in the center of the rug, in his hat, the shaggy iron-gray brows twitching slightly above the pebble-colored eyes as he appeared to examine the house with brief deliberation. Then with the same deliberation he turned; the boy watched him pivot on the good leg and saw the stiff foot drag round the arc of the turning, leaving a final long and fading smear. His father never looked at it, he never once looked down at the rug. The Negro held the door. It closed behind them, upon the hysteric and indistinguishable woman-wail. His father stopped at the top of the steps and scraped his boot clean on the edge of it. At the gate he stopped again. He stood for a moment, planted stiffly on the stiff foot, looking back at the house. "Pretty and white, ain't it?" he said. "That's sweat. Nigger sweat. Maybe it ain't white enough yet to suit him. Maybe he wants to mix some white sweat with it."

Two hours later the boy was chopping wood behind the house within which his mother and aunt and the two sisters (the mother and aunt, not the two girls, he knew that; even at this distance and muffled by walls the flat loud voices of the two girls emanated an incorrigible idle inertia) were setting up the stove to prepare a meal, when he heard the hooves and saw the linen-clad man on a fine sorrel mare, whom he recognized even before he saw the rolled rug in front of the Negro youth following on a fat bay carriage horse—a suffused, angry face vanishing, still at full gallop, beyond the corner of the house where his father and brother were sitting in the two tilted chairs; and a moment later, almost before he could have put the axe down, he heard the hooves again and watched the sorrel mare go back out of the yard, already galloping again.

Then his father began to shout one of the sisters' names, who presently emerged backward from the kitchen door dragging the rolled rug along the ground by one end while the other sister walked behind it.

"If you ain't going to tote, go on and set up the wash pot," the first said.

"You, Sarty!" the second shouted, "Set up the wash pot!" His father appeared at the door, framed against that shabbiness, as he had been against that other bland perfection, impervious to either, the mother's anxious face at his shoulder.

"Go on," the father said. "Pick it up." The two sisters stooped, broad, lethargic; stooping, they presented an incredible expanse of pale cloth and a flutter of tawdry ribbons.

"If I thought enough of a rug to have to git hit all the way from France I wouldn't keep hit where folks coming in would have to tromp on hit," the first said. They raised the rug.

"Abner," the mother said. "Let me do it."

"You go back and git dinner," his father said. "I'll tend to this."

From the woodpile through the rest of the afternoon the boy watched them, the rug spread flat in the dust beside the bubbling wash-pot, the two sisters stooping over it with that profound and lethargic reluctance, while the father stood over them in turn, implacable and grim, driving them though never raising his voice again. He could smell the harsh homemade lye they were using; he saw his mother come to the door once and look toward them with an expression not anxious now but very like despair; he saw his father turn, and he fell to with the axe and saw from the corner of his eye his father raise from the ground a flattish fragment of field stone and examine it and return to the pot, and this time his mother actually spoke: "Abner. Abner. Please don't. Please, Abner."

Then he was done too. It was dusk; the whippoorwills had already begun. He could smell coffee from the room where they would presently eat the cold food remaining from the mid-afternoon meal, though when he entered the house he realized they were having coffee again probably because there was a fire on the hearth, before which the rug now lay spread over the backs of the two chairs. The tracks of his father's foot were gone. Where they had been were now long, water-cloudy scoriations resembling the sporadic course of a lilliputian mowing machine.

It still hung there while they ate the cold food and then went to bed, scattered without order or claim up and down the two rooms, his mother in one bed, where his father would later lie, the older brother in the other, himself, the aunt, and the two sisters on pallets on the floor. But his father was not in bed yet. The last thing the boy remembered was the depthless, harsh silhouette of the hat and coat bending over the rug and it seemed to him that he had not even closed his eyes when the silhouette was standing over him, the fire almost dead behind it, the stiff foot prodding him awake. "Catch up the mule," his father said.

When he returned with the mule his father was standing in the black door, the rolled rug over his shoulder. "Ain't you going to ride?" he said.

"No. Give me your foot."

He bent his knee into his father's hand, the wiry, surprising power flowed smoothly, rising, he rising with it, on to the mule's bare back (they had owned a saddle once; the boy could remember it though not when or where) and with the same effortlessness his father swung the rug up in front of him. Now in the starlight they retraced the afternoon's path, up the dusty road rife with honeysuckle, through the gate and up the black tunnel of the drive to the lightless house, where he sat on the mule and felt the rough warp of the rug drag across his thighs and vanish.

"Don't you want me to help?" he whispered. His father did not answer and now he heard again that stiff foot striking the hollow portico with that wooden and clocklike deliberation, that outrageous overstatement of the weight it carried. The rug, hunched, not flung (the boy could tell that even in the darkness) from his father's shoulder struck the angle of wall and floor with a sound unbelievably loud, thunderous, then the foot again, unhurried and enormous; a light came on in the house and the boy sat, tense, breathing steadily and quietly and just a little fast, though the foot itself did not increase its beat at all, descending the steps now; now the boy could see him.

"Don't you want to ride now?" he whispered. "We kin both ride now," the light within the house altering now, flaring up and sinking, He's coming down the stairs now, he thought. He had already ridden the mule up beside the horse block; presently his father was up behind him and he doubled the reins over and slashed the mule across the neck, but before the animal could begin to trot the hard, thin arm came round him, the hard, knotted hand jerking the mule back to a walk.

In the first red rays of the sun they were in the lot, putting plow gear on the mules. This time the sorrel mare was in the lot before he heard it at all, the rider collarless and even bareheaded, trembling, speaking in a shaking voice as the woman in the house had done, his father merely looking up once before stooping again to the hame he was buckling, so that the man on the mare spoke to his stooping back:

"You must realize you have ruined that rug. Wasn't there anybody here, any of your women..." he ceased, shaking, the boy watching him, the older brother leaning now in the stable door, chewing, blinking slowly and steadily at nothing apparently. "It cost a hundred dollars. But you never had a hundred dollars. You never will. So I'm going to charge you twenty bushels of corn against your crop. I'll add it in your contract and when you come to the commissary you can sign it. That won't keep Mrs. De Spain quiet but maybe it will teach you to wipe your feet off before you enter her house again."

Then he was gone. The boy looked at his father, who still had not spoken or even looked up again, who was now adjusting the logger-head[5] in the hame.

"Pap," he said. His father looked at him—the inscrutable face, the shaggy brows beneath which the gray eyes glinted coldly. Suddenly the boy went toward him, fast, stopping as suddenly. "You done the best you could!" he cried. "If he wanted hit done different why didn't he wait and tell you how? He won't git no twenty bushels! He won't git none! We'll gether hit and hide hit! I kin watch..."

"Did you put the cutter back in that straight stock[6] like I told you?"

"No sir," he said.

"Then go do it."

That was Wednesday. During the rest of that week he worked steadily, at what was within his scope and some which was beyond it, with an industry that did not need to be driven nor even commanded twice; he had this from his mother, with the difference that some at least of what he did he liked to do, such as splitting wood with the half-size axe which his mother and aunt had earned, or saved money somehow, to present him with at Christmas. In company with the two older women (and on one afternoon, even one of the sisters), he built pens for the shoat and the cow which were a part of his father's contract with the landlord, and one afternoon, his father being absent, gone somewhere on one of the mules, he went to the field.

They were running a middle buster[7] now, his brother holding the plow straight while he handled the reins, and walking beside the straining mule, the rich black soil shearing cool and damp against his bare ankles, he thought Maybe this is the end of it. Maybe even that twenty bushels that seems hard to have to pay for just a rug will be a cheap price for him to stop forever and always from being what he used to be; thinking, dreaming now, so that his brother had to speak sharply to him to mind the mule: Maybe he even won't collect the twenty bushels.

Maybe it will all add up and balance and vanish—corn, rug, fire; the terror and grief, the being pulled two ways like between two teams of horses—gone, done with for ever and ever.

Then it was Saturday; he looked up from beneath the mule he was harnessing and saw his father in the black coat and hat. "Not that," his father said. "The wagon gear." And then, two hours later, sitting in the wagon bed behind his father and brother on the seat, the wagon accomplished a final curve, and he saw the weathered paintless store with its tattered tobacco and patent-medicine posters and the tethered wagons and saddle animals below the gallery. He mounted the gnawed steps behind his father and brother, and there again was the lane of quiet, watching faces for the three of them to walk through. He saw the man in spectacles sitting at the plank table and he did not need to be told this was a Justice of the Peace; he sent one glare of fierce, exultant, partisan defiance at the man in collar and cravat now, whom he had seen but twice before in his life, and that on a galloping horse, who now wore on his face an expression not of rage but of amazed unbelief which the boy could not have known was at the incredible circumstance of being sued by one of his own tenants, and came and stood against his father and cried at the justice: "He ain't done it! He ain't burnt..."

"Go back to the wagon," his father said.

"Burnt?" the Justice said. "Do I understand this rug was burned too?"

"Does anybody here claim it was?" his father said. "Go back to the wagon." But he did not, he merely retreated to the rear of the room, crowded as that other had been, but not to sit down this time, instead, to stand pressing among the motionless bodies, listening to the voices:

"And you claim twenty bushels of corn is too high for the damage you did to the rug?"

"He brought the rug to me and said he wanted the tracks washed out of it. I washed the tracks out and took the rug back to him."

"But you didn't carry the rug back to him in the same condition it was in before you made the tracks on it."

His father did not answer, and now for perhaps half a minute there was no sound at all save that of breathing, the faint, steady suspiration of complete and intent listening.

"You decline to answer that, Mr. Snopes?" Again his father did not answer. "I'm going to find against you, Mr. Snopes, I'm going to find that you were responsible for the injury to Major de Spain's rug and hold you liable for it. But twenty bushels of corn seems a little high for a man in your circumstances to have to pay. Major de Spain claims it cost a hundred dollars. October corn will be worth about fifty cents. I figure that if Major de Spain can stand a ninety-five dollar loss on something he paid cash for, you can stand a five-dollar loss you haven't earned yet. I hold you in damages to Major de Spain to the amount of ten bushels of corn over and above your contract with him, to be paid to him out of your crop at gathering time. Court adjourned."

It had taken no time hardly, the morning was but half begun. He thought they would return home and perhaps back to the field, since they were late, far behind all other farmers. But instead his father passed on behind the wagon, merely indicating with his hand for the older brother to follow with it, and he crossed the road toward the blacksmith shop opposite, pressing on after his father, overtaking him, speaking, whispering up at the harsh, calm face beneath the weathered hat: "He won't git no ten bushels neither. He won't git one. We'll..." until his father glanced for an instant down at him, the face absolutely calm, the grizzled eyebrows tangled above the cold eyes, the voice almost pleasant, almost gentle:

"You think so? Well, we'll wait till October anyway."

The matter of the wagon—the setting of a spoke or two and the tightening of the tires—did not take long either, the business of the tires accomplished by driving the wagon into the spring branch behind the shop and letting it stand there, the mules nuzzling into the water from time to time, and the boy on the seat with the idle reins, looking up the slope and through the sooty tunnel of the shed where the slow hammer rang and where his father sat on an upended cypress bolt, easily, either talking or listening, still sitting there when the boy brought the dripping wagon up out of the branch and halted it before the door.

"Take them on to the shade and hitch," his father said. He did so and returned. His father and the smith and a third man squatting on his heels inside the door were talking, about crops and animals; the boy, squatting too in the ammoniac dust and hoof-parings and scales of rust, heard his father tell a long and unhurried story out of the time before the birth of the older brother even when he had been a professional horse trader. And then his father came up beside him where he stood before a tattered last year's circus poster on the other side of the store, gazing rapt and quiet at the scarlet horses, the incredible poisings and convolutions of tulle and tights and the painted leer of comedians, and said, "It's time to eat."

But not at home. Squatting beside his brother against the front wall, he watched his father emerge from the store and produce from a paper sack a segment of cheese and divide it carefully and deliberately into three with his pocket knife and produce crackers from the same sack. They all three squatted on the gallery and ate, slowly, without talking; then in the store again, they drank from a tin dipper tepid water smelling of the cedar bucket and of living beech trees. And still they did not go home. It was a horse lot this time, a tall rail fence upon and along which men stood and sat and out of which one by one horses were led, to be walked and trotted and then cantered back and forth along the road while the slow swapping and buying went on and the sun began to slant westward, they—the three of them—watching and listening, the older brother with his muddy eyes and his steady, inevitable tobacco, the father commenting now and then on certain of the animals, to no one in particular.

It was after sundown when they reached home. They ate supper by lamplight, then, sitting on the doorstep, the boy watched the night fully accomplished, listening to the whippoorwills and the frogs, when he heard his mother's voice: "Abner! No! No! Oh, God. Oh, God. Abner!" and he rose, whirled, and saw the altered light through the door where a candle stub now burned in a bottle neck on the table and his father, still in the hat and coat, at once formal and burlesque as though dressed carefully for some shabby and ceremonial violence, emptying the reservoir of the lamp back into the five-gallon kerosene can from which it had been filled, while the mother tugged at his arm until he shifted the lamp to the other hand and flung her back, not savagely or viciously, just hard, into the wall, her hands flung out against the wall for balance, her mouth open and in her face the same quality of hopeless despair as had been in her voice. Then his father saw him standing in the door.

"Go to the barn and get that can of oil we were oiling the wagon with," he said. The boy did not move. Then he could speak.

"What..." he cried "What are you..."

"Go get that oil," his father said. "Go."

Then he was moving, running outside the house, toward the stable: this the old habit, the old blood which he had not been permitted to choose for himself, which had been bequeathed him willy nilly and which had run for so long (and who knew where, battening on what of outrage and savagery and lust) before it came to him. I could keep on, he thought. I could run on and on and never look back, never need to see his face again. Only I can't. I can't, the rusted can in his hand now, the liquid sploshing in it as he ran back to the house and into it, into the sound of his mother's weeping in the next room, and handed the can to his father.

"Ain't you going to even send a nigger?" he cried. "At least you sent a nigger before!"

This time his father didn't strike him. The hand came even faster than the blow had, the same hand which had set the can on the table with almost excruciating care flashing from the can toward him too quick for him to follow it, gripping him by the back of the shirt and on to tiptoe before he had seen it quit the can, the face stooping at him in breathless and frozen ferocity, the cold, dead voice speaking over him to the older brother who leaned against the table, chewing with that steady, curious, sidewise motion of cows: "Empty the can into the big one and go on. I'll ketch up with you."

"Better tie him to the bedpost," the brother said.

"Do like I told you," the father said. Then the boy was moving, his bunched shirt and the hard, bony hand between his shoulder-blades, his toes just touching the floor, across the room and into the other one, past the sisters sitting with spread heavy thighs in the two chairs over the cold hearth, and to where his mother and aunt sat side by side on the bed, the aunt's arms about his mother's shoulders.

"Hold him," the father said. The aunt made a startled movement. "Not you," the father said. "Lennie. Take hold of him. I want to see you do it." His mother took him by the wrist. "You'll hold him better than that. If he gets loose don't you know what he is going to do? He will go up yonder." He jerked his head toward the road. "Maybe I'd better tie him."

"I'll hold him," his mother whispered.

"See you do then." Then his father was gone, the stiff foot heavy and measured upon the boards, ceasing at last.

Then he began to struggle. His mother caught him in both arms, he jerking and wrenching at them. He would be stronger in the end, he knew that. But he had no time to wait for it. "Lemme go!" he cried. "I don't want to have to hit you!"

"Let him go!" the aunt said. "If he don't go, before God, I am going up there myself!"

"Don't you see I can't?" his mother cried. "Sarty! Sarty! No! No! Help me, Lizzie!"

Then he was free. His aunt grasped at him but was too late. He whirled, running, his mother stumbled forward on to her knees behind him, crying to the nearer sister: "Catch him, Net! Catch him!" But that was too late too, the sister (the sisters were twins, born at the same time, yet either of them now gave the impression of being, encompassing as much living meat and volume and weight as any other two of the family) not yet having begun to rise from the chair, her head, face, alone merely turned, presenting to him in the flying instant an astonishing expanse of young female features untroubled by any surprise even, wearing only an expression of bovine interest. Then he was out of the room, out of the house, in the mild dust of the starlit road and the heavy rifeness of honeysuckle, the pale ribbon unspooling with terrific slowness under his running feet, reaching the gate at last and turning in, running, his heart and lungs drumming, on up the drive toward the lighted house, the lighted door. He did not knock, he burst in, sobbing for breath, incapable for the moment of speech; he saw the astonished face of the Negro in the linen jacket without knowing when the Negro had appeared.

"De Spain!" he cried, panted. "Where's..." then he saw the white man too emerging from a white door down the hall. "Barn!" he cried. "Barn!"

"What?" the white man said. "Barn?"

"Yes!" the boy cried. "Barn!"

"Catch him!" the white man shouted.

But it was too late this time too. The Negro grasped his shirt, but the entire sleeve, rotten with washing, carried away, and he was out that door too and in the drive again, and had actually never ceased to run even while he was screaming into the white man's face.

Behind him the white man was shouting, "My horse! Fetch my horse!" and he thought for an instant of cutting across the park and climbing the fence into the road, but he did not know the park nor how high the vine-massed fence might be and he dared not risk it. So he ran on down the drive, blood and breath roaring;

presently he was in the road again though he could not see it. He could not hear either: the galloping mare was almost upon him before he heard her, and even then he held his course, as if the urgency of his wild grief and need must in a moment more find him wings, waiting until the ultimate instant to hurl himself aside and into the weed-choked roadside ditch as the horse thundered past and on, for an instant in furious silhouette against the stars, the tranquil early summer night sky which, even before the shape of the horse and rider vanished, strained abruptly and violently upward: a long, swirling roar incredible and soundless, blotting the stars, and he springing up and into the road again, running again, knowing it was too late yet still running even after he heard the shot and, an instant later, two shots, pausing now without knowing he had ceased to run, crying "Pap! Pap!," running again before he knew he had begun to run, stumbling, tripping over something and scrabbling up again without ceasing to run, looking backward over his shoulder at the glare as he got up, running on among the invisible trees, panting, sobbing, "Father! Father!"

At midnight he was sitting on the crest of a hill. He did not know it was midnight and he did not know how far he had come. But there was no glare behind him now and he sat now, his back toward what he had called home for four days anyhow, his face toward the dark woods which he would enter when breath was strong again, small, shaking steadily in the chill darkness, hugging himself into the remainder of his thin, rotten shirt, the grief and despair now no longer terror and fear but just grief and despair. Father. My father, he thought. "He was brave!" he cried suddenly, aloud but not loud, no more than a whisper: "He was! He was in the war! He was in Colonel Sartoris' cav'ry!" not knowing that his father had gone to that war a private in the fine old European sense, wearing no uniform, admitting the authority of and giving fidelity to no man or army or flag, going to war as Malbrouck[8] himself did: for booty—it meant nothing and less than nothing to him if it were enemy booty or his own.

The slow constellations wheeled on. It would be dawn and then sun-up after a while and he would be hungry. But that would be tomorrow and now he was only cold, and walking would cure that. His breathing was easier now and he decided to get up and go on, and then he found that he had been asleep because he knew it was almost dawn, the night almost over. He could tell that from the whippoorwills. They were everywhere now among the dark trees below him, constant and inflectioned and ceaseless, so that, as the instant for giving over to the day birds drew nearer and nearer, there was no interval at all between them. He got up. He was a little stiff, but walking would cure that too as it would the cold, and soon there would be the sun. He went on down the hill, toward the dark woods within which the liquid silver voices of the birds called unceasing—the rapid and urgent beating of the urgent and quiring heart of the late spring night. He did not look back.

Questions:

1. What is the nature of the story's conflict? How does each of the story's six scenes serve to reveal, clarify, and intensify the conflict?
2. What seems to motivate Abner's violent, antisocial behavior? Why does he try to make his son Sarty an accomplice to the burning of Major de Spain's barn?Why does Sarty finally defy him and try to warn Major de Spain?
3. What comments does the story offer about the social, moral ,and economic values of the old and the new South?

注　释

1. hermetic meal：罐装肉。
2. Colonel Sartoris：沙多里斯上校，福克纳所虚构的杰弗逊（Jefferson）镇上的名人，内战中的南军军官。穷白人斯诺普斯家族也住此镇。两个家族多次出现于福克纳的其他作品中。

3. Provost's man：宪兵。

4. Blue or gray：兰色和灰色分别是内战中北军和南军的军服颜色，这里指北军和南军。

5. Logger-head：马颈轭的一部分。

6. Straight stock：犁。

7. Middle buster：犁的一种。

8. Malbrouck：马尔布鲁克，18世纪法国民谣《马尔布鲁克已赴战场》（*Malbrouck Has Gone to the War*）中的人物，常被看成约翰·丘吉尔（John Churchill），即第一代马尔伯勒（Marborough）公爵。他靠非凡的军事才能从士兵升至中将，曾率领英军战胜法王路易十四，是历史名将之一。但他也是一个有争议的人物，被指责为谋乱反上，唯利是图。

He (the writer) must teach himself that the basest of all things is to be afraid; and, teaching himself that, forget it forever leaving no room in his workshop for anything but the old verities and truths lacking which any story is ephemeral and doomed—love and honor and pity and pride and compassion and sacrifice.

—William Faulkner

第九章
厄内斯特·海明威Ernest Hemingway

作者简介

厄内斯特·海明威（Ernest Hemingway，1899—1961），出生在一个医生家庭，中学毕业后当过记者。记者职业对文字、文体的要求对他日后作品的内容和文风产生影响。第一次世界大战中，海明威参加志愿救护车队，在意大利前线被弹片击中负伤。这段战争生活为他的名著《永别了，武器》和许多短篇小说提供了极其宝贵的素材。战后，他去巴黎做记者，结识了旅欧美国作家斯泰因、庞德等人，在写作上得到了他们的帮助。

1925年，他发表短篇小说集《在我们的时代里》（*In Our Time*），以简洁的文笔和不露情感的表达风格开始引起人们的注意。第一部长篇小说《太阳照样升起》（*The Sun Also Rises*，1926）描写一战后流落巴黎、迷惘空虚、靠酗酒和情爱的刺激寻求精神慰籍的美国青年，奠定了海明威在文坛的地位，使他成为"迷惘一代[1]"作家的代表。另一部长篇小说《永别了，武器》（*A Farewell to Arms*,1929）通过主人公亨利在一战中负伤、恋爱、最后爱人难产而死的故事描述战争给人带来的无法弥合的心灵创伤和传统信念的破灭。此外，《丧钟为谁而鸣》（*For Whom the Bell Tolls*，1940）以西班牙内战为背景，刻画主人公为信念理想而战，在残酷的战斗中勇敢地面对死亡。最后一部体现他人生价值和行为准则的《老人与海》（*The Old Man and the Sea*，1952）为他赢得了1954年的诺贝尔文学奖。1961年，他不堪病痛的折磨自杀而死。

海明威是20世纪一位十分重要的作家。他既描写人类面临的灾难和虚空，又表现人在逆境下的勇气和尊严。他的主人公可能迷惘绝望，但在痛苦面前却谈笑若定，决不放弃男子汉的气度。海明威的文风继承了马克·吐温的口语体传统，文字质朴无华，但蕴涵却极为丰富。借用他本人的比喻：冰山移动的尊严在于它仅有八分之一露出水面。

赏　析

本文故事发生的场景是一个西班牙小咖啡馆，情节的发展围绕老年顾客，中年侍者和年轻侍者等三人。老年人富有但生活对他毫无意义，他自杀未遂，靠酗酒排遣空虚；年轻人自信，自私，急于下班和妻子亲热；而中年人对人生深有所悟，因而富有同情心，知道青春、爱情、激情转瞬即逝，代之而来的是绝望和虚无，人需要勇气和自尊，否则只能用睡眠和忘却来填补对黑暗和空寂的恐惧。

小说的自然主义（naturalism）描写和象征表现（symbolism）合璧天成。中年侍者表达了人对光明、整洁和秩序的需要，以及对黑暗和虚无的莫名焦虑。光明与黑暗，秩序与混沌，存在与虚无形成象征对比，而特定的环境和三个人的不同处世态度进一步引发联想，使故事细节产生象征意义。黑暗和混沌象征虚无、绝望、衰老与死亡，而被黑暗和混沌所包围和侵蚀的一点点光明和整洁则象征抵御黑暗和虚无的心灵慰藉。这样，笼罩在老者头上的树叶光影及灯光、黑暗中闪亮的士兵铜领章、整洁的小店、保持整洁的老者、老者的贪杯和对生存的恐惧（尽管富有却要自杀）、年轻人的邋遢服务（将酒撒出）、他对老者心态的无动于衷、对青春、情爱和工作的盲目自信以及中年人对老者的理解同情，甚至对士兵的情欲和年轻妻子偷情的玩笑话，都因此各具象征意义。年轻孕育衰老、情欲是无欲的前奏、秩序的偶然存在于混沌的必然[2]、生命回避不了死亡、存在的意识来自虚无的体验。所有这些似乎都包孕在完全自然主义的写实中。这是典型的海明威风格。

故事的一个重要主题——虚无（nada/nothing）[3]在侍者讨论老者为何自杀时就已提及，随后通过中年侍者的自白进一步明晰，这不是个人对某个具体事物的恐惧（“It was not fear or dread”），而是由于意识到人生悬系于未知，个人生存的秩序感和行为完全没有真实依据，个人只能孤独面对变动不居的周遭关系，而又退避无门，因而产生一种不可名状的恐惧和焦虑感。老者的财富不能帮他解脱空虚，他想以死结束痛苦却没有成功，只得找个整洁明亮的环境来逃避虚无。年轻人不理解老者求死和酗酒的行为，没有意识到老者的今天可能就是自己的明天，但他是否多少意识到他所自信的情爱和工作却都仅以靠不住的青春来维系呢？中年人推人及己感悟到人生的无奈和飘忽无着，虚无其实是唯一真实可靠的体验。老者寻求一个整洁明亮的小店，借酒浇愁；年轻人浑浑噩噩，得过且过；中年人则在心灵中寻求秩序、准则以及生存意义，保留一片心中整洁明亮的空间，关爱理解他人，体验虚无并勇敢地面对虚无。

A Clean, Well-lighted Place

It was late and every one had left the cafe except an old man who sat in the shadow the leaves of the tree made against the electric light. In the day time the street was dusty; but at night the dew settled the dust and the old man liked to sit late because he was deaf and now at night it was quiet and he felt the difference. The two waiters inside the cafe knew that the old man was a little drunk, and while he was a good client they knew that if he became too drunk he would leave without paying, so they kept watch on him.

"Last week he tried to commit suicide," one waiter said.

"Why?"

"He was in despair."

"What about?"

"Nothing."

How do you know it was nothing?"

"He has plenty of money."

They sat together at a table that was close against the wall near the door of the cafe and looked at the terrace where the tables were all empty except where the old man sat in the shadow of the leaves of the tree that moved slightly in the wind. A girl and a soldier went by in the street. The street light shone on the brass number on his collar. The girl wore no head covering and hurried beside him.

"The guard will pick him up[4]," one waiter said.

"What does it matter if he gets what he's after[5]?"

"He had better get off the street now. The guard will get him. They went by five minutes ago."

The old man sitting in the shadow rapped on his saucer with his glass. The younger waiter went over to him.

"What do you want?"

The old man looked at him. "Another brandy," he said.

"You'll be drunk," the waiter said. The old man looked at him. The waiter went away.

"He'll stay all night," he said to his colleague. "I'm sleepy now. I never get into bed before three o'clock. He should have killed himself last week."

The waiter took the brandy bottle and another saucer from the counter inside the cafe and marched out to the old man's table. He put down the saucer and poured the glass full of brandy.

"You should have killed yourself last week," he said to the deaf man. The old man motioned with his finger." A little more," he said. The waiter poured on into the glass so that the brandy slopped over and ran down the stem into the top saucer of the pile[6]. "Thank you," the old man said. The waiter took the bottle back inside the cafe. He sat down at the table with his colleague again.

"He's drunk now," he said.

"He's drunk every night."

"What did he want to kill himself for?"

"How should I know."

"How did he do it?"

"He hung himself with a rope."

"Who cut him down[7]?"

"His niece."

"Why did he do it?"

"Fear his soul[8]."

"How much money has he got?"

"He's got plenty."

"He must be eighty years old."

"Anyway I should say he was eighty."

"I wish he would go home. I never get to bed before three o'clock. What kind of hour is that to go to bed?"

"He stays up because he likes it."

"He's lonely. I'm not lonely. I have a wife waiting in bed for me."

"He had a wife once too.[9]"

"A wife would be no good to him now.[10]"

"You can't tell. He might be better with a wife."

"His niece looks after him."

"I know. You said she cut him down."

"I wouldn't want to be that old. An old man is a nasty thing."

"Not always. This old man is clean. He drinks without spilling. Even now, drunk. Look at him."

"I don't want to look at him. I wish he would go home. He has no regard for those who must work."

The old man looked from his glass across the square, then over at the waiters.

"Another brandy," he said, pointing to his glass. The waiter who was in a hurry came over.

"Finished," he said, speaking with that omission of syntax stupid people employ when talking to drunken people or foreigners. "No more tonight. Close now."

"Another," said the old man.

"No. Finished." The waiter wiped the edge of the table with a towel and shook his head.

The old man stood up, slowly counted the saucers[11], took a leather coin purse from his pocket and paid for the drinks, leaving half a peseta[12] tip.

The waiter watched him go down the street, a very old man walking unsteadily but with dignity,.

"Why didn't you let him stay and drink?" the unhurried waiter asked. They were putting up the shutters. "It is not half-past two."

"I want to go home to bed."

"What is an hour?[13]"

"More to me than to him[14]."

"An hour is the same."

"You talk like an old man yourself. He can buy a bottle and drink at home."

"It's not the same."

"No, it is not," agreed the waiter with a wife. He did not wish to be unjust. He was only in a hurry.

"And you? You have no fear of going home before your usual hour [15]?"

"Are you trying to insult me?"

"No, hombre[16], only to make a joke."

"No," the waiter who was in a hurry said, rising from putting on the metal shutters. "I have confidence. I am all confidence."

"You have youth, confidence, and a job," the older waiter said. "You have everything.[17]"

"And what do you lack?"

"Everything but work.[18]"

" You have everything I have."

"No. I have never had confidence and I'm not young."

"Come on. Stop talking nonsense and lock up."

"I am of those who like to stay late at the cafe," the older waiter said. "With all those who do not want to go to bed. With all those who need a light for the night."

"I want to go home and into bed."

"We are of two different kinds," the older waiter said. He was now dressed to go home. "It is not only a question of youth and confidence although those things are very beautiful. Each night I am reluctant to close up because there may be some one who needs the cafe."

"Hombre, there are bodegas open all night long."

"You do not understand. This is a clean and pleasant cafe. It is well lighted. The light is very good and also, now, there are shadows of the leaves."

"Good night," said the younger waiter.

"Good night," the other said. Turning off the electric light he continued the conversation with himself. It is the light of course but it is necessary that the place be clean and light. You do not want music. Certainly you do not want music. Nor can you stand before a bar with dignity although that is all that is provided for these hours. What did he fear? It was not fear or dread. It was a nothing that he knew too well. It was all a nothing and a man was nothing too. It was only that and light was all it needed and a certain cleanness and order. Some lived in it and never felt it but he knew it all was nada[19] y[20] pues[21] nada y pues nada. Our nada who art in nada, nada be thy name thy kingdom nada thy will be nada in nada as it is in nada. Give us this nada our daily nada and nada us our nada as we nada our nadas and nada us not into nada but deliver us from nada; pues nada. Hail nothing full of nothing, nothing is with thee. He smiled and stood before a bar with a shining steam pressure coffee machine.

"What's yours?" asked the barman.

"Nada."

"Otro loco mas," said the barman and turned away.

"A little cup," said the waiter.

The barman poured it for him.

"The light is very bright and pleasant but the bar is unpolished," the waiter said.

The barman looked at him but did not answer. It was too late at night for conversation.

"You want another copita[24]?" the barman asked.

"No, thank you," said the waiter and went out. He disliked bars and bodegas. A clean, well-lighted cafe was a very different thing. Now, without thinking further, he would go home to his room. He would lie in the bed and finally, with daylight, he would go to sleep. After all, he said to himself, it is probably only insomnia. Many must have it.

Questions:

1. How do you interpret the irony of the title after reading the story?
2. Do you think youth and confidence can help one withstand the metaphorical dark? Why or why not?
3. The older waiter said to the younger waiter. "We are of two different kinds." In what way do you think they are different?

注　释

1. "迷惘的一代"（the Lost Generation）泛指第一次世界大战后的一代人，也特指一批美国作家。他们是一次大战时的青年，20年代开始在文坛崭露头角。女作家斯泰因曾对海明威说："你们都是迷惘的一代。"海明威把这句话用作小说《太阳照常升起》的卷首语。这一代人的迷惘是因为他们的传统民主自由的价值观与战后的世界格格不入，加之美国受政府推行的"恢复常态”政策影响，使这些青年感到美国冷酷无情，只重实际利益，让这些青年与美国在精神上疏远起来。这些作家包括海明威、菲茨杰拉德、约翰·多斯·帕索斯等多人，但他们并没有形成统一的文学流派，而是各自保留自己的独立风格。

2. 根据热力学第二定律，宇宙中一切事物必然由有序向无序转化。

3. “虚无”(nothing)在这里带有海德格尔存在主义色彩，海德格尔的虚无(nothingness)涵盖一切强加于人的外在力量，它无边无际、莫可名状，而个体却又无从逃避。理性秩序在它面前无能为力，由此而来的是恐惧感。正是在这种生活现实中，个体体验存在，体验自身的有限，生命转瞬即逝。对死亡不可避免的恐惧是因为死亡必须由个人面对而不能像其他行为那样可由他人代劳，面对死亡的意识影响人生的各种抉择。但是人无论怎么选择都会对自己的选择产生自责，因此自责感是人生不可逃避的现实。另一方面，人的各种思想意图总是具有外部世界中相应的事物，而恐惧感在外部世界却不存在对应事物，它只是虚无，表明世界没有任何个人行为可以依托的实在基础。而正是在这种无法摆脱的焦虑状态中，人需要构建确立自身真实的良心依托，并据此做出负责的人生选择，关爱整个世界。

4. The guard will pick him up.(宵禁)卫兵会逮捕他的。

5. What does it matter if he gets what he's after? 如果他能得到他想得到的东西，这又有什么关系呢？这句话暗示那个士兵想满足自己的欲望。

6.The waiter poured on into the glass so that the brandy slopped over and ran down the stem into the top saucer of the pile. 这个句子表现年轻侍者很不耐烦，有意将酒倒出杯子外。这一邋遢行为与后面年长侍者谈到老者的整洁、从不将酒洒出相对比。

7. Who cut him down? 是谁把绳子切断救他下来的？

8. Fear for his soul. 为他的灵魂不能得救而担心。基督教认为自杀是一种犯罪，是对上帝行为的干预。

9. He had a wife once too. 这里年长侍者暗示老者也曾拥有年轻侍者现在拥有的一切。

10. A wife would be no good to him now. 这里年轻侍者认为这样一把年纪就是有妻子也没有用。
11. The old man...counted the saucers...顾客根据碟子的数量计算自己要了多少杯酒。
12. peseta: 比塞塔(西班牙货币单位)
13. What is an hour ? 晚一个小时有什么关系呢?
14. More to me than to him. 对我比对他重要得多。
15. You have no fear going home before your usual hour? 这里年长侍者开了个玩笑，暗示如果回家比平时早可能会撞见妻子偷情。
16. hombre:(西班牙文)男人，老兄。
17. "You have youth, confidence, and a job." ... "You have everything." 这里年长侍者暗示年轻人拥有青春，因此拥有自信。
18. Everything but work: 除了工作什么都没有。这里年长侍者暗示没有了青春也就没有了自信,而青春的逝去恰恰是自己无法掌控的。
19. nada:(西班牙文)不存在，没有，虚无。
20. y:(西班牙文)和，所以，那么。
21. pues:(西班牙文)既然，那么。
22. Our nata who art ...nothing is with thee.这是一段摹仿祷告词，其中的名词和动词等实词被"虚无"取代，表明一切事物和行为都是虚无。
23. Otro loco mas.(西班牙文)又一个疯子。这句话表明以世人的标准来看，年长侍者的行为是"不正常"的。
24. copita: 西班牙等地所产浅黄色或深褐色葡萄酒。

A man can be destroyed but not defeated.

The dignity of movement of an iceberg is due to only one-eighth of it being above water.

—Ernest Hemingway

第十章
索而·贝娄Saul Bellow

作者简介

索尔·贝娄(Saul Bellow,1915—),犹太裔小说家。生于加拿大的魁北克,9岁时随父母移居芝加哥。先后就读于芝加哥大学和西北大学,1937年获社会学和人类学学士学位。同年进入威斯康辛大学研究生院专攻人类学,但因想当作家而于年底退学。回芝加哥后一边从事教学等工作,一边练习写作。1941年发表第一篇作品。二战期间服务于美国商船队。之后15间在纽约大学和普林斯顿大学等校教书,并去巴黎生活和游历。1962年返回芝加哥,执教于芝加哥大学。第一部长篇小说《晃来晃去的人》(*Dangling Man*)1944年问世。其他小说有《受害人》(*The Victim*, 1947)、《奥吉.玛琪历险记》(*The Adventures of Augie March*,1953)、《只争朝夕》(Seize the Day)、《雨王汉德森》(*Henderson the Rain King*,1959)、《赫尔索格》(*Herzog*,1964)、《赛拉姆先生的行星》(*Mr.Sammler' s Planet*,1970)、《洪堡的礼物》(*Humbolt' s Gift*,1975)、《院长的十二月》(*The Dean' s December*,1982)、《更多人死于悲痛》(*More Die of Heartbreak*,1987)、《盗窃》(*The Theft*,1989)、《真实的》(The Actual,1997)等。其中《奥吉·玛琪历险记》、《赫尔索格》和《赛拉姆先生的行星》获全国图书奖,《洪堡的礼物》获普利策奖。他的短篇小说收录于《莫斯比的回忆及其他故事》(*Mosby' s Memories and Other Stories*,1968)等集子里。他还发表过《最后的分析》(*The Last Analysis*,1965)等剧本。他的作品多以芝加哥和纽约为背景,以犹太人为主要人物,描写现代社会里精神与物质的矛盾以及现代人对自我的寻找。1976年获诺贝尔文学奖。

赏 析

《寻找格林先生》选自《莫斯比的回忆及其他故事》，是贝娄的一篇代表性短篇小说。篇首引语——“凡你当做的事，要尽力去做……”——点明作品主题。在故事中，主人公格利伯(Grebe)不畏困难，竭尽全力，终于找到了格林(Green)。贝娄认为，尽管人不能改变自己的命运，但凭着他的人性，他能以某种方式超越异化的环境。格利伯寻找格林的努力，显示了他丰富的人性以及他寻找自我、超越异化的强烈愿望和坚定意志。在表现这一主题的过程中，作品也以同情的笔触描写了下层人，尤其是黑人的困苦与心态。

格利伯寻找格林的情节被雷诺(Raynor)与格利伯的谈话分成两部分，而他们的谈话又被斯台卡(Staita)夫人的抗议分成两部分。这一状况形成了作品的基本结构，同时也体现了作者的风格特点，即对照与反讽的使用。作品中那充满贫穷与敌意的现实，对于雷诺办公室里那夹杂着拉丁语和哲学思辨的谈话来说，既是一种对照，又是一种反讽。故事的基本情节就具有反讽意味。居然难以向急需救济的人发送支票，这自然是件咄咄怪事。格利伯的名字也包含对照与讽刺。“Grebe”是一种以其复杂的求偶舞而著称的鸟，而格利伯却是个单身汉。这种鸟成双成对地生活在自己的地盘内，而格利伯为了工作不得不走进与他格格不入的区域。较值得注意的是，在作品中，格利伯努力寻找的格林始终没有出现。这一与作品的写实倾向相对照的空缺，有效地连接起故事里的事件，激发着格利伯和读者的想象。

Looking for Mr.Green

Whatsoever thy hand findeth to do, do it with thy might...[1]

Hard work? No, it wasn't really so hard. He wasn't used to walking and stair-climbing, but the physical difficult of his new job was not what George Grebe felt most. He was delivering relief checks in the Negro district, and although he was a native Chicagoan this was not a part of the city he knew much about—

it needed a depression to introduce him to it. No, it wasn't literally hard work, not as reckoned in foot-pounds, but yet he was beginning to feel the strain of it, to grow aware of its peculiar difficulty. He could find the streets and numbers, but the clients were not where they were supposed to be, and he felt like a hunter inexperienced in the camouflage of his game. It was an unfavorable day, too—fall, and cold, dark weather, windy. But, anyway, instead of shells in his deep trenchcoat pocket he had the cardboard of checks, punctured for the spindles of the file, the holes reminding him of the holes in player-piano paper. And he didn't look much like a hunter, either; his was a city figure entirely, belted up in this Irish conspirator's coat. He was slender without being tall, stiff in the back, his legs looking shabby in a pair of old tweed pants gone through and fringy at the cuffs. With this stiffness, he kept his head forward, so that his face was red from the sharpness of the weather; and it was an indoors sort of face with gray eyes that persisted in some kind of thought and yet seemed to avoid definiteness of conclusion. He wore sideburns that surprised you somewhat by the tough curl of the blond hair and the effect of assertion in their length. He was not so mild as he looked, nor so youthful; and nevertheless there was no effort on his part to seem what he was not. He was an educated man; he was a bachelor; he was in some ways simple; without lushing, he liked a drink; his luck had not been good. Nothing was deliberately hidden.

He felt that his luck was better than usual today. When he had reported for work that morning he had expected to be shut up in the relief office at a clerk's job, for he had been hired downtown as a clerk, and he was glad to have, instead, the freedom of the streets and welcomed, at least at first, the vigor of the cold and even the blowing of the checks. It was true that it was a city job; nobody expected you to push too hard at a city job. His supervisor, that young Mr.Raynor, had practically told him that. Still, he wanted to do well at it. For one thing, when he knew how quickly he could deliver a batch of checks, he would know also how much time he could expect to clip for himself. And then, too, the clients would be waiting for their money. That was not the important consideration, though it certainly mattered to him. No, but he wanted to do well, simply for doing-well's sake, to acquit himself decently of a job because he so rarely had a job to do that required just this sort of energy. Of this peculiar energy he now had a superabundance; once it had started to flow, it flowed all too heavily. And, for the time being anyway, he was balked. He could not find Mr. Green.

So he stood in his big-skirted trenchcoat with a large envelope in his hand and papers showing from his pocket, wondering why people should be so hard to locate who were too feeble or sick to come to the station to collect their own checks. But Raynor had told him that tracking them down was not easy at first and had offered him some advice on how to proceed. "If you can see the postman, he's your first man to ask, and your best bet. If you can't connect with him, try the stores and trades-people around. Then the janitor and the neighbors. But you'll find the closer you come to your man the less people will tell you. They don't want to tell you anything."

"Because I'm a stranger."

"Because you're white. We ought to have a Negro doing this, but we don't at the moment, and of course you've got to eat, too, and this is public employment. Jobs have to be made. Oh, that holds for me too. Mind you, I'm not letting myself out. I've got three years of seniority on you, that's all. And a law degree. Otherwise, you might be back of the desk and I might be going out into the filed this cold day. The same dough pays us both and for the same, exact, identical reason. What's my law degree got to do with it? But you have to pass out these checks, Mr.Grebe, and it'll help if you're stubborn, so I hope you are."

"Yes, I'm fairly stubborn."

Raynor sketched hard with an eraser in the old dirt of his desk, left-handed, and it said, "Sure, what else can you answer to such a question. Anyhow, the trouble you're going to have is that they don't like to give information about anybody. They think you're a plain-clothes dick or an installment collector, or summons-server or something like that. Till you've been seen around the neighborhood for a few months and people know you're only from the relief."

It was dark, ground-freezing, pre-Thanksgiving weather; the wind player hob with the smoke, rushing down, and Grebe office. And no one would admit knowing Green. It was past three o'clock and the postman had made his last delivery. The nearest grocer, himself a Negro, had never heard the name Tulliver Green, or said he hadn't. Grebe was inclined to think that it was true, that he had in the end convinced the man that he wanted only to deliver a check. But he wasn't sure. He needed experience in interpreting looks and sighs and, even more, the will not to be put off or denied hand even the force to bully if need be... If the grocer did know, he had got rid of him easily. But since most of his trade was with reliefers, why should he prevent the delivery of a check? Maybe Green, or Mr.Green, if there was a Mrs.Green, patronized another grocer. And was there a Mrs.Green? It was one of Grebe's great handicaps that he hadn't looked at any of the case records. Raynor should have let jim read files for a few hours. But he apparently saw no need for that, probably considering the job unimportant. Why prepare systematically to deliver a few checks?

But now it was time to look for the janitor. Grebe took in the building in the wind and gloom of the late November day—trampled, frost-hardened lots on one side; on the other, an automobile junk yard and then the infinite work of Elevated frames[2], weak-looking, gaping with rubbish fires; two sets of learning brick porches three stories high and a fight of cement stairs to the cellar. Descending, he entered the underground passage, where he tried the doors until one opened and he found himself in the furnace room. There someone rose toward him and approached, scraping on the coal grit and bending under the canvas-jacketed pipes.

"Are you the janitor?"

"What do you want?"

"I'm looking for a man who's supposed to be living here. Green."

"What Green?"

"Oh, you maybe have more than one Green?" said Grebe with new, pleasant hope. "This is Tulliver Green."

"I don't think I can help you, mister. I don't know any."

"A crippled man."

The janitor stood bent before him. Could it be that he was crippled? Oh, God! what if he was. Grebe's gray eyes sought with excited difficulty to see. But no, he was only very short and stooped. A head awakened from meditation, a strong-haired beard, low, wide shoulders. A staleness of sweat and coal rose from his black shirt and the staleness of sweat and coal rose from his black shirt and the burlap sack he wore as an apron.

"Crippled how?"

Grebe thought and then answered with the light voice of unmixed candor, "I don't know. I've never seen him." This was damaging, but his only other choice was to make a lying guess, and he was not up to it. "I'm delivering checks for the relief to shut-in cases. If he weren't crippled he'd come to collect himself. That's why I said crippled. Bedridden, chair-ridden—is there anybody like that?"

This sort of frankness one of Grebe's oldest talents, going back to childhood. But it gained him nothing here.

"No suh. I've got four buildin's same as this that I take care of. I don't know all the tenants, leave alone the tenants. The rooms turn over so fast, people movin'in and out every day. I can't tell you."

The janitor opened his grimy lips but Grebe did not hear him in the piping of the valves and the consuming pull of air to flame in the body of the furnace. He knew, however, what he had said.

Once more in the cold air and early darkness he made the short circle from the cellarway to the entrance crowded between the brickwork pillars and began to climb to the third floor. Pieces of plaster ground under his feet; strips of brass tape from which the carpeting had been torn away marked old boundaries at the sides. In the passage, the cold reached him worse than in the street; it touched him to the bone. The hall toilets ran like springs. He thought grimly as he heard the wind burning around the building with a sound like that of the furnace, that this was a great piece of constructed shelter. Then he struck a match in the gloom and searched for names and numbers among the writings and scribbles on the walls. He saw WHOODY-DOODY GO TO JESUS, and zigzags, caricatures, sexuals, and curses. So the sealed rooms of pyramids were also decorated, and the caves of human dawn.

The information on his card was, TULLIVER GREEN—APT 3D. There were no names, however, and no numbers. His shoulders drawn up, tears of cold in his eyes, breathing vapor, he went the length of the corridor and told himself that if he had been lucky enough to have the temperament for it he would bang on one of the doors and bawl out "Tulliver Green!" until he got results. But it wasn't in him to make an uproar and he continued to burn matched, passing the light over the walls. At the rear, in a corner off the hall, he discovered a door he had not seen before and he thought it best to investigate. It sounded empty when he knocked, but a young Negress answered, hardly more than a girl. She opened only a bit, to guard the warmth of the room.

"Yes suh?"

"I'm from the district relief station on Prairie Avenue. I'm looking for a man named Tulliver Green to give him his check. Do you know him?"

No, she didn't; but he thought she had not understood anything of what he had said. She had a dream-bound, dream-blind face, very soft and black, shut off. She wore a man's jacket and pulled the ends together at her throat. Her hair was parted in three directions, at the sides and transversely, standing up at the front in a dull puff.

"Is there somebody around here who might know?"

"I just' taken this room las' week."

He observed that she shivered, but even her shiver was somnambulistic and there was no sharp consciousness of cold in the big smooth eyes of her handsome face.

"All right, miss, thank you. Thanks," he said, and went to try another place.

Here he was admitted. He was grateful, for the room was warm. It was full of people, and they were silent as he entered—ten people, or a dozen, perhaps more, sitting on benches like a parliament. There was no light, properly speaking, but a tempered darkness that the window gave, and everyone seemed to him enormous, the men padded out in heavy work clothes and winter coats, and the women huge, too, in thick sweaters, hats, and old furs. And, besides, bed and bedding, a black cooking range, a piano piled towering to the ceiling with papers, a dining-room table of the old style of prosperous Chicago. Among these people Grebe, with his heightened fresh color and his smaller stature, entered like a schoolboy. Even though he was met with smiles and good will, he knew, before a single word was spoken, that all the currents ran against him and that he would make no headway. Nevertheless he began. "Does anybody here know how I can deliver a check to Mr. Tulliver Green?"

"Green?" It was the man that had let him in who answered. He was in short sleeves, in a checkered shirt, and had a queer, high head, profusely overgrown and long as a shako; the veins entered it strongly from his forehead. "I never heard mention of him. Is this where he live?"

"This is the address they gave me at the station. He's a sick man, and he'll need his check. Can't anybody tell me where to find him?"

He stood his ground and waited for a reply, his crimson wool scarf wound about his neck and drooping outside his trenchcoat, pockets weighted with the block of checks and official forms. They must have realized that he was not a college boy employed afternoons by a bill collector, trying foxily to pass for a relief clerk, recognized that he was an older man who knew himself what need was, who had had more than average seasoning in hardship. It was evident enough if you looked at the marks under his eyes and at the sides of his mouth.

"Anybody know this sick man?"

"No suh." On all sides he saw heads shaken and smiles of denial. No on knew. And maybe it was true, he considered, standing silent in the earthen, musky human gloom of the place as the rumble continued. But he could never really be sure.

"What's the matter with this man?" said shako-head.

"I've never seen him. All I can tell you is that he can't come in person for his money. It's my first day in this district."

"Maybe they given you the wrong number?"

"I don't believe so. But where else can I ask about him?" He felt that this persistence amused them deeply, and in a way he shared their amusement that he should stand up so tenaciously to them. Though smaller, though slight, he was his own man, he retracted nothing about himself, and he looked back at them, gray-eyed, with amusement and also with a sort of courage. On the bench some man spoken in his throat, the words impossible to catch, and a woman answered with a wild, shrieking laugh, which was quickly cut off.

"Well, so nobody will tell you?"

"Ain't nobody who knows."

"At least, if he lives here, he pays rent to someone. Who manages the building?"

"Greatham Company. That's on Thirty-ninth Street."

Grebe wrote it in his pad. But, in the street again, a sheet of wind-driver paper clinging to his leg while he deliberated what direction to take next, it seemed a feeble lead to follow. Probably this Green didn't rent a flat, but a room. Sometimes there were as many as twenty people in an apartment; the real-estate agent would know only the lessee. And not even the agent could tell you who the renters were. In some places the beds were even used in shifts, watchmen or jitney drivers or short-order cooks in night joints turning out after a day's sleep and surrendering their beds to a sister, a nephew, or perhaps a stranger, just off the bus. There were large numbers of newcomers in this terrific, blight-bitten portion of the city between Cottage Grove and Ashland, wandering from house to house and room to room. When you saw them, how could you know them? They didn't carry bundles on their backs or look picturesque. You only saw a man, a Negro, walking in the street or riding in the car, like everyone else, with his thumb closed on a transfer. And therefore how were you supposed to tell? Grebe thought the Greatham agent would only laugh at his question.

But how much it would have simplified the job to be able to say that Green was old, or blind, or consumptive. An hour in the files, taking a few notes, and he needn't have been at such a disadvantage. When Raynor gave him the block of checks he asked, "How much should I know about these people?" Then Raynor had looked as though he were preparing to accuse him of trying to make the job more important than it was. He smiled, because by then they were on fine terms, but nevertheless he had been getting ready to say something like that when the confusion began in the station over Staika and her children.

Grebe had waited a long time for this job. It came to him through the pull of an old schoolmate in the Corporation Counsel's office, never a close friend, but suddenly sympathetic and interested—pleased to show, moreover, how well he had done, how strongly he was coming on even in these miserable times. Well, he was coming through strongly, along with the Democratic administration itself. Grebe had gone to see him in City Hall, and they had had a counter lunch or beers at least once a month for a year, and finally it had been possible to swing the job. He didn't mind being assigned the lowest clerical grade, not even being a messenger, though Raynor thought he did.

This Raynor was an original sort of guy and Grebe had taken to him immediately. As was proper on the first day, Grebe had come early, but he waited long, for Raynor was late. At last he darted into his cubicle of an office as though he had just jumped from one of those hurting huge red India Avenue cars. His thin, tough face was wind-stung and he was grinning and saying something breathlessly to himself. In his hat, a small fedora, and his coat, the velvet collar a neat fit about his neck, and his silk muffler that set off the nervous twist of his chin, he swayed and turned himself in his swivel chair, feet leaving the ground; so that he pranced a little as he sat. Meanwhile he took Grebe's measure out of his eyes, eyes of an unusual vertical length and slightly sardonic. So the two men sat for a while, saying nothing, while the supervisor raised his hat from his miscombed hair and put it in his lap. His cold-darkened hands were not clean. A steel beam passed through the little makeshift room, from which machine belts once had hung. The building was an old factory.

"I'm younger than you; I hope you won't find it hard taking orders from me," said Raynor. "But I don't make then up, either. You're how old, about?"

"Thirty-five."

"And you thought you'd be inside doing paper work. But it so happens I have to send you out."

"I don't mind."

"And it's mostly a Negro load we have in this district."

"So I thought it would be."

"Fine. You'll get along. C'est un bon boulot.[3] Do you know French?"

"Some."

"I thought you'd be a university man."

"Have you been in France?" said Grebe.

"No, that's the French of the Berlitz School. I've been at it for more than a year, just as I'm sure people have been, all over the world, office boys in China and braves in Tanganyika. In fact, I damn well know it. Such is the attractive power of civilization. It's overrated, but what do you want? Que voulez-vous?[4] I get Le Rire[5] and all the spicy papers, just like in Tanganyika. It must be mystifying, out there. But my reason is that I'm aiming at the diplomatic service. I have a cousin who's a courier, and the way he describes it is awfully attractive. He rides in the wagon-lits and reads books. While we—What did you do before?"

"I sold."

"Where?"

"Canned meat at Stop and Shop. In the basement."

"And before that?"

"Steady work?"

"No, Thursdays and Saturdays. I also sold shoes."

"You've been a shoe-dog too. Well. And prior to that? Here it is in your folder." He opened the record. "Saint Olaf's College, instructor in classical languages. Fellow, University of Chicago, 1926—27. I've had Latin, too. Let's trade quotations—'Dum spiro spero6'"

" 'Da dextram misero.[7]' "

" 'Alea jacta est.[8]' "

" 'Excelsior.[9]' "

Raynor shouted with laughter, and other workers came to look at him over the partition. Grebe also laughed, feeling pleased and easy. The luxury of fun on a nervous morning.

When they were done and no one was watching or listening, Raynor said rather seriously, "What made you study Latin in the first place? Was it for the priesthood?"

"No."

"Just for the hell of it? For the culture? Oh, the things people think they can pull!" He made his cry hilarious and tragic. "I ran my pants off so I could study for the bar, and I've passed the bar, so I get twelve dollars a week more than you as a bonus for having seen life straight and whole. I'll tell you, as a man of culture, that even though nothing looks to be real, and everything stands for something else, and that thing for another thing, and that thing for a still further one—there ain't any comparison between twenty-five and thirty-seven dollars a week, regardless of the last reality. Don't you think that was clear to your Greeks? They were a thoughtful people, but they didn't part with their slaves."

This was a great deal more than Grebe had looked for in his first interview with his supervisor. He was too shy to show all the astonishment he felt. He laughed a little, aroused, and brushed at the sunbeam that covered his head with its dust. "Do you think my mistake was so terrible?"

"Damn right it was terrible, and you know it now that you've had the whip of hard times laid on your back. You should have been preparing yourself for trouble. Your people must have been well off to send you to the university. Stop me, if I'm stepping on your toes. Did your mother pamper you? Did your father give in to you? Were you brought up tenderly, with permission to go and find out what were the last things that everything else stands for while everybody else labored in the fallen world of appearance?"

"Well, no, it wasn't exactly like that." Grebe smiled. The fallen world of appearances! No less. But now it was his turn to deliver a surprise. "We weren't rich. My father was the last genuine English butler in Chicago—"

"Are you kidding?"

"Why should I be?"

"In a livery?"

"In livery. Up on the Gold Last[10]. "

"And he wanted you to be educated like a gentleman?"

"He did not. He sent me to the Armour Institute to study chemical engineering. But when he died I changed schools."

He stopped himself, and considered how quickly Raynor had reached him. In no time he had your valise on the table and all your stuff unpacked. And afterward, in the streets, he was still reviewing how far he might have gone, and how much he might But just then a young woman, one of Raynor's workers, ran into the cubicle exclaiming, "Haven't you heard all the fuss?"

"We haven't heard anything."

"It's Staika, giving out with all her might. The reporters are coming. She said she phoned the papers, and you know she did."

"But what is she up to?" said Raynor.

"She brought her wash and she's ironing it here, with out current, because the relief won't pay her electric bill. She has her ironing board set up by the admitting desk, and her kids are with her, all six. They never are i school more than once a week. She's always dragging them around with her because of her reputation."

"I don't want to miss any of this," said Raynor, jumping up. Grebe, as he followed with the secretary, said, "Who is thin Staika?"

"They call her the 'Blood Mother of Federal Street.' She's a professional donor at the hospitals. I think they pay ten dollars a pint. Of course it's no joke, but she makes a very big thing out of it and she and the kids are in the paper all the time."

A small crowd, staff and clients divided by a plywood barrier, stood in the narrow space of the entrance, and Staika was shouting in a gruff, mannish voice, plunging the iron on the board and slamming it on the metal rest.

"My father and mother came in a steerage, and I was born in our house, Raynor by Huron. I'm no dirty immigrant. I'm a U.S. Citizen. My husband is a gassed veteran from France with lungs weaker'n paper, that hardly can he go to the toilet by himself. These six children of mine, I have to buy the shoes for their feet with my own blood. Even a lousy little white Communion necktie, that's a couple of drops of blood; a little piece of mosquito veil for my Vadja so she won't be ashamed in church for the other girls, they take my blood for it by Goldblatt. That's how I keep goin'. A fine thing if I had to depend on the relief. And there's plenty of people on the rolls—fakes! There's nothin' they can't get, that can go and wrap bacon at Swift and Armour any time. They're lookin' for them by the Yards. They never have to be out of work. Only they rather lay in their lousy beds and eat the public's money." She was not afraid, in a predominantly Negro station, to shout this way about Negroes.

Grebe and Raynor worked themselves forward to get a closer view of the woman. She was flaming with anger and with pleasure at herself, broad and huge, a gold-headed woman who wore a cotton cap laced with pink ribbon. She was barelegged and had on black gym shoes, her Hoover apron was open and her great breasts, not much restrained by a man's undershirt, hampered her arms as she worked at the kid's dress on the ironing board. And the children, silent and white, with a kind of locked obstinacy, in sheepskins and lumberjackets, stood behind her. She had captured the station, and the pleasure this gave her was enormous. Yet her grievances were true grievances. She was telling the truth. But she behaved like a liar. The look of her small eyes was hidden, and while she raged she also seemed to be spinning and planning.

"They send me out college case workers in silks pants to talk me out of what I got comin'. Are they better'n me? Who told them? Fire them. Let'em go and get married, and then you won't have to cut electric from people's budget."

The chief supervisor, Mr. Ewing, couldn't silence her and he stood with folded arms at the head of his staff, bald, bald-headed, saying to his subordinates like the ex-school principal he was, "Pretty soon she'll be tired and go."

"No she won't," said Raynor to Grebe. "She'll get what she wants. She knows more about the relief even then Ewing. She's been on the rolls for years, and she always gets what she wants because she puts on a noisy show. Ewing knows it. He'll give in soon. He's only saving face. If he gets bad publicity, the Commissioner'll have him on the carpet, downtown. She's got him submerged; she'll submerged everybody in time, and that includes nations and governments."

Grebe replied with his characteristic smile, disagreeing completely. Who would take Staika's orders, and what changes could her yelling ever bring about?

No, what Grebe saw in her, the power that made people listen, was that her cry expressed the war of flesh and blood, perhaps turned a little crazy and certainly ugly, on this place and this condition. And at first, when he went out, the spirit of Staika somehow presided over the whole district for him, and it took color from her; he saw her color, in the sporty curb fires, and the fires under the EI, the straight alley of flamy gloom. Later, too, when he went into a tavern for a shot of rye, the sweat of beer, association with West Side Polish streets, made him think of her again.

He wiped the corners of his mouth with his muffler, his handkerchief being inconvenient to reach for, and went out again to get on with the delivery of his checks. The air bit cold and hard and a few flakes of snow formed near him. A train struck by and left a quiver in the frames and a bristling icy hiss over the rails.

Crossing the street, he descended a flight of board steps into a basement grocery, setting off a little bell. It was a dark, long store and it caught you with its stinks of smoked meat, soap, dried peaches, and fish. There was a fire wrinking and flapping in the little stove, and the proprietor was waiting, an Italian with a long, hollow face and stubborn bristles. He kept his hands warm under his apron.

No, he didn't know Green. You knew people but not names. The same man might not have the same name twice. The police didn't know, either, and mostly didn't care. When somebody was shot or knifed they took the body away and didn't look for the murderer. In the first place, nobody would tell them anything.

So they made up a name for the coroner and called it quits. And in the second place, they didn't give a goddamn anyhow. But they couldn't get to the bottom of a thing even if they wanted to. Nobody would get to know even a tenth of what went on among these people. They stabbed and stole, they did every crime and abomination you ever heard of, men and men, women and women, parents and children, worse than the animals. They carried on their own way, and the horrors passed off like a smoke. There was never anything like it in the history of the whole world.

It was a long speech, deepening with every word in its fantasy and passion and becoming increasingly senseless and terrible: a swarm amassed by suggestion and invention, a huge, hugging, despairing knot, a human wheel of heads, legs, bellies, arms, rolling through his shop.

Grebe felt that he must interrupt him. He said sharply, "What are you talking about! All I asked was whether you knew this man."

"You probably don't want to believe this. But suppose it's true?"

"All the same," said Grebe, "there must be a way to find a person."

The Italian's close-spaced eyes had been queerly concentrated, as were his muscles, while he ad leaned across the counter trying to convince Grebe. Now he gave up the effort and sat n down on his tool. "Oh—I suppose. Once in a while. But I been telling you, even the cops don't get anywhere."

"They're always after somebody. It's not the same thing."

"Well, keep trying if you want. I can't help you."

But he didn't keep trying. He had no more time to spend on Green. He slipped Green's check to the back of the block. The next name on the list was FIELD WINSTON.

He found the back-yard bungalow without the least trouble; it shared a lot with another house, a few feet of yard between. Grebe knew these two-shack arrangements. They had been built in vast numbers in the days before the swamps were filed and the streets raised, and they were all the same—a boardwalk along the fence, well under street level, three or four ball-headed posts for clothesliness, greening wood, dead shingles, and a long, long flight of stairs to the rear door.

A twelve-year-old boy let him into the kitchen, and there the old man was sitting by the table in a wheel chair.

"Oh, it's d'Government man," he said to the boy when Grebe drew out his checks. "Go bring me my box of papers." He cleared a space on the table.

"Oh, you don't have to go to all that trouble," said Grebe. But Field laid out his papers: Social Security card, relief certification, letters from the state hospital in Manteno, and a naval discharge dated San Diego, 1920.

"That's plenty," Grebe said. "Just sign."

"You got to know who I am," the old man said. "you're from the Government. It's not your check, it's a Government check and you got no business to hand it over till everything is proved."

He loved the ceremony of it, and Grebe made no more objections. Field emptied his box and finished out the circle of cards and letters.

"There's everything I done and been. Just the death certificate and they can close book on me." He said this with a certain happy pride and magnificence. Still he did not sign; he merely held the little pen upright on the gold-green corduroy of his thigh. Grebe did not hurry him. He felt the old man's hunger for conversation.

"I got to get better coal," he said. "I send my little gran'son to the yard with my order and they fill his wagon with screening. The stove ain't made for it. It fall through the grate. The order says Franklin County egg-size coal."

"I'll report it and see what can be done."

"Nothing can be done, I expect. You know and I know. There ain't no little ways to make things better, and the only big thing is money. That's the only sunbeams, money. Nothing is black where it shines, and the only place you see black is where it ain't shining. What we colored have to have is our own rich.

There ain't no other way."

Grebe sat, his reddened forehead bridged levelly by his close-cut hair and his cheeks lowered in the wings of his collar—the caked fire shone hard within the isinglass-and-iron frames but the room was not comfortable—sat and listened while the old man unfolded his scheme. This was to create on Negro millionaire a month by subscription. One clever, good-hearted young fellow elected every month would sign a contract to use the money to start a business employing Negroes. This would be advertised by chain letters and word of mouth, and every Negro wage earner would contribute a dollar a month. Within five years there would be sixty millionaires.

"That'll fetch respect," he said with a throat-stopped sound that came out like a foreign syllable. "You got to take and organize all the money that gets thrown away on the policy wheel and horse race. As long as they can take it away from you, they got no respect for you. Money, that's d'sun of human kind!" Field was a Negro of mixed blood, perhaps Cherokee, or Natchez; his skin was reddish. And he sounded, speaking about a golden sun in this dark room, and looked, shaggy and slab-headed, with the mingled blood of his face and board lips, the little pen still upright in his hand, like one of the underground kings of mythology, old judge Minos himself.

And now he accepted the check and signed. Not to soil the slip, he held it down with his knuckles. The table budged and creaked, the center of the gloomy, heathen midden of the kitchen covered with bread, meat, and cans, and the scramble of papers.

"Don't you think my scheme'd work?"

"It's worth thinking about. Something ought to be done, I agree."

"It'll work if people will do it. That's all. That's the only thing, any time. When they understand it in the same way, all of them."

"That's true," said Grebe, rising. His glance met the old man's.

"I know you got to go," he said. "Well, God bless you, boy, you ain't been sly with me. I can tell it in a minute."

He went back through the buried yard. Someone nursed a candle in a shed, where a man unloaded kindling wood from a sprawl-wheeled baby buggy and two voices carried on a high conversation. As he came up the sheltered passage he heard the hard boost of the wind in the branches and against the house fronts, and then, reaching the sidewalk, he saw the needle-eye red of cable towers in the open icy height hundreds of feet above the river and factories—those keen points. From here, his view was obstructed all the way to the South Branch and its timber banks, and the cranes beside the water. Rebuilt after the Great Fire, this part of the city was, not fifty years later, in ruins again, factories boarded up, buildings deserted or fallen, gaps of prairie between. But it wasn't desolation that this made you feel, but rather a faltering of organization that set free a huge energy, an escaped, unattached, unregulated power from the giant raw place. Not only must people feel it but, it seemed to Grebe, they were compelled to match it. In their very bodies. He no less than others, he realized. Say that his parents had been servants in their time, whereas he was not supposed to be one. He thought that they had never done any service like this, which no one visible asked for, and probably flesh and blood could not even perform. Nor could anyone show why it should be performance would lead. That did not mean that he wanted to be released from it, he realized with a grimly pensive face. On the contrary. He had something to do. To be compelled to feel this energy and yet have no task to do—that was horrible; that was suffering; he knew what that was. It was now quitting time. Six o'clock. He could go home if he liked, to his room, that is, to wash in hot water, to pour a drink, lie down on his quilt, read the paper, eat some liver paste on crackers before going out to dinner. But to think of this actually made him feel a little sick, as though he had swallowed hard air. He had six checks left, and he was determined to deliver at least one of these: Mr. Green's check.

So he started again. He had four of five dark blocks to go, past open lots, condemned houses, old foundations, closed schools, black churches, mounds, and he reflected that there must be many people alive who had once seen the neighborhood rebuilt and new. Now there was a second layer of ruins; centuries of history accomplished through human massing. Numbers had given the place forced growth; enormous numbers had also broken it down. Objects once so new, so concrete that it could have occurred to anyone they stood for other things, had crumbled. Therefore, reflected Grebe, the secret of them was out. It was that they stood for themselves by agreement, and were natural and not unnatural by agreement, and when the things themselves collapsed the agreement became visible. What was it, otherwise, that kept cities from looking peculiar? Rome, that was almost permanent, did not give rise to thoughts like these. And was it abidingly real? But in Chicago, where the cycles were so fast and the familiar died out, and again rose changed, and died again in thirty years, you saw the common agreement or covenant, and you were forced to think about appearance and realities. (He remembered Raynor and he smiled. Raynor was a clever boy.) Once you had grasped this, a great many things became intelligible. For instance, why Mr. Field should conceive such a scheme. Of course, if people were to agree to create a millionaire, a real millionaire would come into existence. And if you wanted to know how Mr. Field was inspired to think of this, why, he had within sight of his kitchen window the chart, the very bones of a successful scheme—the EI with its blue and green confetti of signals. People consented to pay dimes and ride the crash-box cars, and so it was a success. Yet how absurd it looked; how little reality there was to start with. And yet Yerkes[11] , the great financier who built it, had known that he could get people to agree to do it. Viewed as itself, what a scheme of a scheme it seemed, how close to an appearance. Then why wonder at Mr. Field's idea? He had grasped a principle. And then Grebe remembered, too, that Mr. Yerkes had established the Yerkes Observatory and endowed it with millions. Now how did the nation come to him in his New York museum of a palace or his Aegean-bound yacht to give money to astronomers? Was he awed by the success of his bizarre enterprise and therefore ready to spend money to find out where in the university being and seeming were identical? Yes, he wanted to know what abides; and whether flesh is Bible grass[12], and he offered money to be burned in the fire of suns. Okay, then, Grebe thought further, these things exist because people consent to exist with them—we have got so far—and also there is a reality which doesn't depend on consent but within which consent is a game. But what about need, the need that keeps so many vast thousands in position? You tell me that, you private little gentleman and decent soul—he used these words against himself scornfully. Why is the consent given to misery? And why so painfully ugly? Because there is something that is dismal and permanently ugly? Here he sighed and gave it up, and thought it was enough for the present moment that he had a real check in his pocket for a Mr. Green who must be real beyond question. If only his neighborhood didn't think they had to conceal him.

This time he stopped at the second floor. He struck a match and found a door. Presently a man answered his knock and Grebe had the check ready and showed it even before he began. "Does Tulliver Green live here? I'm from relief."

The man narrowed the opening and spoken to someone at his back.

"Does he live here?"

"Uh-uh. No."

"Or anywhere in this building? He's a sick man and he can't come for his dough." He exhibited the check in the light, which was smoky—the air smelled of charred lard—and the man held off the brim of his cap to study it.

"Uh-uh. Never seen the name."

He seemed to think, but it was Grebe's impression that he was simply waiting for a decent interval to pass.

"No, suh. Nobody I ever see."

"I've been looking for this man all afternoon."—Grebe spoke out with sudden force—"and I'm going to have to carry this check back to the station. It seems strange not to be able to find a person give him something when you're looking for him for a good reason. I suppose if I had bad news for him I'd find him quick enough."

There was a responsive motion in the other man's face. "That's right, I reckon."

"It almost doesn't do any good to have a name if you can't be found by it. It doesn't stand for anything. He might as well not have any," he went on, smiling. It was as much of a concession as he could make of his desire to laugh.

"Well, now, there's a little old knot-back man I see once in a while. He might be the one you lookin' for Downstairs."

"Where? Right side or left? Which door?"

"I don't know which. This-face little knot-back with a stick."

But no one answered at any of the doors on the first floor. He went to the end of the corridor, searching by matchlight, and found only a stairless exit to the yard, a drop of about six feet. But there was a bungalow near the alley, an old house like Mr. Field's. To jump was unsafe. He ran from the front door, through thc underground passage and into the yard. The place was occupied. There was a light through the curtains, upstairs. The name on the ticket under the broken, scoop-shaped mailbox was Green! He exultantly rang the bell and pressed against the locked door. Then the lock clicked faintly and a long staircase opened before him. Someone was slowly coming down—a woman. He had the impression in the weak light that she was shaping her hair as she came, making herself presentable, for he saw her arms raised. But it was for support that they were raised; she was feeling her way downward, down the wall, stumbling. Next he wondered about the pressure of her feet on the treats; she did not seem to be wearing shoes. And it was a freezing stairway. His ring had got her out of bed, perhaps, and she had forgotten to put them on. And then he saw that she was not only shoeless but naked; she was entirely naked, climbing down while she talked to herself, a heavy woman, naked and drunk. She blundered into him. The contact of her breasts, though they touched only his coat, made him go back against the door with a blind shock. See what he had tracked down, in his hunting game!

The woman was saying to herself, furious with insult, "So I cain't—k, huh? I'll show that son-of-a-bitch kin I, cain't I."

What should he do now? Grebe asked himself. Why, he should go. He should turn away and go. He couldn't talk to this woman. He couldn't keep her standing naked in the cold. But when he tried he found himself unable to turn away.

He said, "Is this where Mr. Green lives?"

At last she turned her furious drunken glance on him. "What do you want?"

Again her eyes wandered from him; there was a dot of blood in their enraged brilliance. He wondered why she didn't feel the cold.

"I'm from the relief."

"Awright, what?"

"I've got a check for Tulliver Green."

This time she heard and put out her hand.

"No, no, for Mr. Green. He's got to sign," he said. How was he going to get Green's signature tonight!

"I'll take it. He cain't."

He desperately shook his head, thinking of Mr. Field's precautions about identification. "I can't let you have it. It's for him. Are you Mrs.Green?"

"Maybe I is, and maybe I ain't. Who want to know?"

"Is he upstairs?"

"Awright. Take it up yourself, you goddamn fool."

Sure, he was a goddamn fool. Of course he could not go up because Green would probably be drunk and naked, too. And perhaps he would appear on the landing soon. He looked eagerly upward. Under the light was a high narrow brown wall. Empty! It reminded empty!

"Hell with you, then!" he heard her cry. To deliver a check for coal and clothes, he was keeping her in the cold. She did not feel it, but his face was burning with frost and self-ridicule. He backed away from her.

"I'll come tomorrow, tell him."

"Ah, hell with you. Don't never come. What you doin' here in the nighttime? Don't come bake." She yelled so that he saw the breadth of her tongue. She stood astride in the long cold box of the hall and held on to the banister and the wall. The bungalow itself was shaped something like a box, a clumsy, high box pointing into the freezing air with its sharp, wintry lights.

"If you are Mrs. Green, I'll give you the check." he said, changing his mind.

"Give here, then." She took it, took the pen offered with it in her left hand, and tried to sigh the receipt on the wall. He looked around, almost as though to see whether his madness was being observed, and came near believing someone was standing on a mountain of used tires in the auto-junking shop next door.

"But are you Mrs.Green?" he now thought to ask. But she was already climbing the stairs with the check, and it was too late, if he had made an error, if he was now in trouble, to undo the thing. But he wasn't going to worry about it. Though she might not be Mrs.Green, he was convinced that Mr. Green was upstairs. Whoever she was, the woman stood for Green, whom he was not to see this time. Well, you silly bastard, he said to himself, so you think you found him. So what? Maybe you really did find him—what of it? But it was important that there was a real Mr.Green whom they could not keep him from reaching because he seemed to come as an emissary from hostile appearances. And though the self-ridicule was slow to diminish, and his face still blazed with it, he had, nevertheless, a feeling of elation, too. "For after all," he said, "he could be found!"

Questions:

1. Each of the characters in the story—Grebe, Raynor, the janitor, Staika, the Italian grocer, Field—either explicitly or implicitly embodies a certain attitude toward life. Can you identify or characterize these attitudes?
2. Why does it become increasingly important to Grebe that there is "a real Mr. Green" ?
3. What are we to make of the story's conclusion? Is it optimistic, pessimistic, or simply ambivalent and inclusive?

注　释

1. Whatsoever thy hand findeth to do, do it with thy might... "凡你当做的事，要尽力去做"。引自《旧约全书·传道书》第9章第10节。
2. Elevated frame：即elevated railroad, 高粱轨道。
3. C'est un bon boulot.［法语］那是份好工作。
4. Que voulez-vous?［法语］您想要什么？
5. Le Rire：法国一幽默杂志名。
6. Dum spiro spero：［拉丁语］我活着就会产生希望。
7. Da dextram misero.［拉丁语］向不幸者伸出你的右手。
8. Alea jacta est. 骰子已掷。
9. Excelsior. 再高一点。
10. Gold Coast：芝加哥北部的一富人区。
11. Yerkes：耶基斯（Charles Tyson Yerkes, 1837—1905），金融家，曾把兴建芝加哥公共交通的各公司联合成辛迪加。德莱赛以他的生活为素材创作了《金融家》、《巨人》、《斯多噶》。
12. Flesh is Bible grass：《圣经》里有血肉之躯犹如会干枯的草，唯有上帝的话恒久不变的说法。见《旧约全书·以赛亚书》第40章第6节和第8节。

Why should wretched man need power or wish to inflate himself with imaginary glory? If this is what power signifies it can only be vanity to suffer from impotence. On the nobler assumption he should have at least sufficient power to overcome ignominy to complete his life.

—Saul Bellow